ESCAPE FROM LONDON
Idyllic Places to Live within an Hour of the Capital

ESCAPE FROM LONDON
Idyllic Places to Live within an Hour of the Capital
DENNIS WATTS

First published in Great Britain in 2004 by
Allison & Busby Limited
Bon Marche Centre
241-251 Ferndale Road
London SW9 8BJ
http://www.allisonandbusby.com

A catalogue record for this book is available from
the British Library.

ISBN 0 7490 0624 2

Printed and bound in Wales
by Creative Print & Design, Ebbw Vale

DENNIS WATTS is a property consultant, advising corporations on housing their employees across the UK.

Acknowledgements

Thanks go to the very helpful staff of all the council offices of the areas covered and to some estate agents.

House price information is reproduced under licence from HM Land Registry.

Special thanks to my wife, Rita, who assisted with research and proof reading and to my son, David, for much advice and assistance with the use of information technology.

Contents

A note to the reader:

Although plunging straight into the chapters covering particular counties is tempting, Part One provides very useful background information and advice that is not always repeated in the later chapters on individual counties.

Before deciding where to visit and view properties, reading whole county and district sections of Part Two will be more helpful than reading only the entry for a particular place.

This should ensure your house-hunting is a success.

PART ONE

Introduction

Making the Decision

London has many attractions. But needs can change with circumstances. Up to a quarter of a million people leave the London area each year to be replaced by those keen on its attractions. This mobility and migration maintains the capital's vitality. For the individual or family living in or near the capital, though, the time comes to seek improved quality of life and changes to life-style.

Many decisions must be made. Much information gathered. Many areas must be visited and researched. Wrong choices could become expensive and distressing mistakes. This book aims to help with the decisions and save time. Obviously, the advice cannot be totally comprehensive on such a vast area and changing situation but a starting point is provided here.

Looking at the area around London on a map is daunting. The total area within reasonable commuting distance is over 5,000 square miles. This provides plenty of choice but knowing where to start is a problem.

Asking friends or relatives for advice can help but there are many misconceptions about places based on rumour, hearsay and age-old prejudice. Estate agents and local councils often tend to emphasise the positive – after all, that is what they are paid to do. Visiting areas yourself is the best procedure. Decide where to start with guidance from the following chapters. This saves time, petrol, wear on the car, stress and frustration. Avoiding just *one* wasted trip to unsuitable areas could save more than the price of this book in travelling costs alone!

Some assumptions have been made. The escapee will be moving from London, Greater London or moving from elsewhere in the UK to work in London and will want to:

- be in a pleasant rural area or within five minutes' walk of open countryside

- avoid urban areas and large towns

- have access to a choice of, preferably, good schools, a variety of shops and services and leisure facilities

- have a garden of a reasonable size

- have space to park one or more cars without the problems experienced in so many areas of London.

You Are Not Alone

You are probably acutely aware of the circumstances that prompt you to move out but these are some of the categories of people thinking in the same way and it may be useful to be aware of them:

Couples living in London who are about start a family and need a larger home, garden, access to parkland or countryside and good schools.

Expanding families looking for larger, better value housing.

Prospering families who may have inherited money from relatives and be able to afford a substantial property with more space.

Second home hunters wanting weekends not far from a main home in London.

Relocating workers who may be required to move out of London by relocating employers.

'Down-sizers': those, usually in older age groups, who may want to cash in some of the equity in their highly priced London home and are willing to down-size to a rural property.

Anyone seeking a more relaxing, healthier way of life in tranquil surroundings.

The Flow of People To and From the City

The social make-up of rural settlements near London has been changing over recent centuries. It is sometimes suggested that the 'original' village occupants resent the arrival of newcomers from the city with their higher purchasing power pushing up house prices. However, vast numbers of the original rural dwellers migrated to the cities during the Industrial Revolution. Although the working conditions were often poor in city factories, the *increasing* rural population would have found it difficult to make a living if they had remained in their villages. Urbanisation has now given way to *counter*-urbanisation and many are returning to villages where their ancestors lived. This point is often ignored – most of the population lived in villages a few centuries ago. At that time some were wealthier than others and could afford to buy houses rather than rent them. This is the situation now, as some of the urban population *return* to a rural environment and can afford to buy their homes.

Another point is the considerable benefit to local property owners and landowners of providing renovated old properties and new developments for sale at good prices to those moving from London. This can be a great help to farmers who have recently been through difficult times and had their incomes reduced. Plenty have been relieved to sell an old cottage or piece of building land at recently increased prices in order to avoid financial difficulties.

An influx of people with a good level of disposable income must also help the local economies and employment prospects. An example is the increase in customers for produce sold by local farm shops. Local tradespeople providing services to householders also benefit.

Emphasis of this Book

This is not a guide to every single location around London. The emphasis is on:

'Dream property' – typically a detached four bedroom property with garden and garage, either overlooking a rural area or within walking distance of the countryside, yet within reasonably easy reach of the facilities and attractions of London and other urban areas.

Escape from the urban environment, noise and overcrowding of the City and the Greater London area.

Getting away from urban living so concentrating on attractive villages and small towns within reasonable reach of the facilities of a large town as well as commuting to London.

Use of this Book

Plan and enjoy days out looking for places to live. It's important to spend time visiting a variety of areas and going back more than once. Choose a county, find a main town or district within that chapter and plan a route bearing in mind the descriptions. Only the more attractive places to live are covered – on the assumption that when leaving an urban area there is a desire to find a pleasant and picturesque rural place to live.

How to Find a Village or Other Rural Location

Part Two of this book is organised into counties.

Each county chapter is then subdivided into district council or borough council areas. These names tend to be more meaningful and recognisable than postcodes.

Each of the areas has one or more main towns.

Following the information for each town, most of the nearest attractive rural villages and locations are covered.

It will be more helpful to read the chapter on a whole county first when considering an area to visit, but to find a particular village, either look in the appropriate county chapter for the nearest town or use the Place Name Index to go straight to the relevant page.

Detailed maps are not included in this book. To do so would double the size, weight and cost of the book. Excellent detailed maps and road atlases have become available in recent years covering all the areas around London and should be used in conjunction with this book. A detailed place name index occurs at the back of county atlases and can be used with the index at the back of this book. The A to Z series has been expanded to cover very much more than Greater London, and Ordnance Survey publications include a county series of street map atlases with very detailed coverage. Most drivers already have road map atlases to use in planning routes. It would not make sense to try to improve on these.

It is very helpful to have a compass in the car to help navigate an unfamiliar area. Compass directions are used frequently in the entries under the headings of counties and towns.

The Push and Pull Factors

Where to live is one of the most important decisions of your life – similar to choice of partner. This book helps to get you started and saves time but you need to organise the decision making process and do plenty of research to make sure you satisfy the main priorities.

The priorities can be called 'push' and 'pull' factors. These may be familiar from school geography. This is applied geography. Movement (migration) happens for particular reasons.

Push factors are the ones that push you into leaving London or Greater London.

Pull factors attract you to the areas outside Greater London.

In many cases the pull factor is the antithesis of the push factor but there are exceptions. Making a list of each factor and comparing them helps decision-making when applied to particular locations.

Push and Pull Factors and the Family

Ask each member of the household to tick any of the following that apply and add any extras below.

Next, each person should write an index number of 1 to 10 under each factor according to how important the factors are to each of you.

Bear in mind the comparative importance of each of these when visiting areas of interest and viewing property. This should help to clarify thoughts, opinions of family members and decision-making.

Push factors For leaving London or Greater London.	Pull factors That attract you to the rural areas outside Greater London.
Fear of increased crime	Much less crime
Noise	Quieter environment
Air pollution	Cleaner air
Traffic congestion	Less traffic
Congestion charging	No congestion charge
Unsuitable neighbours	More distance from neighbours
Change in neighbourhood community	Better community
Rapid pace of life	Slower pace
Lack of suitable open spaces nearby	Plenty of open country- side accessible nearby
Overcrowding	Uncrowded
Parking problems	Parking within garden
No garage	Garage or garage space
Lack of garden or suffi- cient garden space	Large garden and possi- bly acreage of land
Poor leisure facilities of suitable types	Outdoor activities nearby in pleasant surroundings
Oppressive built-up envi- ronment	Spacious natural sur- roundings

Push factors For leaving London or Greater London.	Pull factors That attract you to the rural areas outside Greater London.
Planned changes to nearby buildings / roads/airport/etc.	Many conservation areas protected from development
Unsatisfactory local schools	Better schools
Living 'over the shop' (at or too near place of work)	Choice of location in relation to workplace
Accommodation too small for family	Larger property cheaper to buy
Employer relocating place of work	Choice of rural location near to new place of work
Cost of living too high	Housing cheaper
Unhealthy environment	More healthy rural area
Stress caused by urban living	Relaxing spacious environment
Life expectancy often less in urban area	Life expectancy usually longer in healthier rural environment
Other:	**Other:**

Recent surveys of people who moved to the country have indicated a longer life expectancy, better health, more relaxed and enjoyable way of life, improved family relationships and even a better sex life! It seems the fresh air, stimulating natural environment and relaxed pace of life have more benefits than might be imagined. After all, plenty of creative minds have found inspiration and stimulation in the excellent rural scenery and surroundings. Some of these authors, poets and composers are mentioned in the chapters on particular areas around Greater London.

Important General Information

Housing

House Prices

A huge advantage for London residents is the higher price usually achievable for property in London compared with similar property in many surrounding areas.

A quite small home in many parts of London may sell for half a million pounds or more but a detached house with garden, garage and off road parking in some rural areas can cost much less and even leave enough over for a small flat near the workplace for use when in the city.

The situation, of course, varies substantially. Surrey, for example is more expensive than most parts of rural Essex.

Prices in the chapters on particular counties are from the Government's Land Registry, published in the second half of 2003. These figures are taken from the prices of property actually sold rather than from the asking prices as in advertised property. They provide a useful approximate guide and a way to compare property prices in particular areas.

Figures are given for administrative districts within each county. This gives an idea of the average price for each type of property rather than misleading figures based on the sale of a few properties in a particular village. Figures are available from the Land Registry for each postcode but these figures are often based on the sale of a small number of properties of a particular type. This can be misleading if, for example, some large, very well-appointed detached houses with large gardens have been sold recently. There may be other, smaller, detached properties coming on the market at much lower prices. This is where the figures provided are useful for an indication of areas to visit.

Accordingly, no attempt has been made to provide figures for every village. The averages provided for each district and for each property type, help to identify affordable areas of interest. The latest situation can then be checked with local estate agents who will, of course, be very pleased to help further.

Buyers always want to know future prices but this is in the realms of predicting horse race winners! Some aspects to consider are the positive and negative effects of proposed new roads and other developments in the area. An area that becomes more accessible for commuting usually experiences more rapid price increases – unless a new road runs past the garden! Future neighbours may be planning to site new houses in their gardens. It is worth enquiring at the local planning offices about their policy on this and your solicitor should find details of any current developments that could affect the property and its value.

Space

Farmhouses, farmworkers cottages and country houses could often take up a reasonable amount of space where it was plentiful in open farmland. This is in contrast to the cramped 20th century housing estates in urban areas, constructed close together with small gardens because the price of land for building has reached such a high level in our small islands. Generally, rural property, therefore, provides the opportunity to find bigger rooms inside and larger gardens outside, particularly older rural dwellings.

Housing Types and Building Materials

A whole book could be written on this topic but to be brief, there is, of course, a wide range of buildings and materials in the large area within an hour's train journey of London.

This is one of the appealing aspects of the area. It is not all built from one type of stone as with some towns and villages in other parts of Britain. In fact, because there is not one obvious ubiquitous building material available locally, this has caused people to be inventive and create a fascinating variety. The following information will be of interest to those seeking a particular type of rural retreat, perhaps significantly different from the familiar brick and concrete of most areas of the capital and Greater London.

Timber Construction

The huge forests that originally existed in the area provided timber for building. This is to be seen in the timber-framed buildings particularly in areas where there is a lack of local stone to be used in construction, such as Essex.

The earliest wooden framed structures were built by inserting supports straight into the soil. Inevitably they rotted and had to be rebuilt repeatedly. A major technical advance was the development of a plinth of stone or bricks to raise the wooden structure clear of damp soil. This extended the life of the building enormously and almost indefinitely, provided it was well maintained. Some of the earliest examples are in Kent where house timbers have been dated from the 13th century using scientific dating techniques.

Even modest cottages were built with plinths protecting the wooden frame from damp resulting in many surviving from the 14th century onwards. Oak was used for the frame. It was used immediately it was cut because seasoned timbers were so hard and difficult to cut. Consequently, as the timbers dried out, they distorted and this helped to give the characterful crooked shapes often seen in old timber framed houses.

Late medieval timber framed houses, particularly in the Weald of Kent and parts of Essex, Surrey and Sussex, were often built in a box shaped frame of timbers with a large open hall. This ran through the house from ground to roof and was used as a general dining area. Each end of the house was completed with two-storey construction. A central fireplace provided heat and the smoke rose to the thatched roof where an opening or simple chimney ventilated it.

Most of these houses have since been redesigned internally to provide more separate rooms but investigation of the roof timbers may show if the house was originally built with an open hall if the timbers are blackened by smoke. The floor was made of compressed soil hardened with animal blood or crushed chalk with sour milk. Fortunately, these floors have since been replaced with more fragrant materials.

Between the thick and sturdy timbers of the box frame, thinner vertical timbers (studding) were installed. Infill panels made the house weatherproof. These panels were often made of wattle and daub. Lengths of split hazel, ash or oak were woven in and out of vertical staves. A mixture of wet clay and other materials, often including cow hair or cow dung, was firmly applied to both sides of the wattle to make up a suitable thickness. A coat of plaster was followed by limewash or ochre. The exposed oak timbers took on a grey appearance and it was only in early Victorian times that it became fashionable to paint them black. Nowadays, some owners of timber-framed houses have reverted to the original charming silvery grey finish.

Some walls have been built of brick between the timbers but brick infilling was most likely to have been used to replace wattle and daub on older houses. An advantage of the wattle and daub, though, is its flexibility. This accommodates the inevitable distortion and subsidence over the centuries better than brick.

Pargetting is sometimes to be seen – where exterior plaster has been moulded into patterns of flowers and foliage or images of people and country scenes. Good examples are to be seen in Saffron Walden, Essex.

'Jettying' is the term given to the overhang of the upper floors on many timber framed houses – particularly those built in the 16th century. The floor joists project out up to a metre from the wall. This provided much more floor space and counterbalanced loads on the floor in the room.

Thatch was the original main roofing material in south-east England where slate or suitable stone was not available and it was very expensive to transport it from distant areas such as parts of Wales. It was only with the coming of the railways that slate became more readily available.

Norfolk reed is generally regarded as the best material for thatch as it can last for 50 years. Straw and lower quality materials may only last 20 years. An attraction is the picturesque appearance – often enhanced with scalloped edging and decorative detail – even including birds and cats made of thatch material. Fire risk is greater with thatch – unless regularly treated with fire-retardants – and it can be more expensive to insure but it certainly acts as a good insulator.

Wealthier house owners replaced thatch with tiles from the 15th century onwards. New roofs built with tiles did not have to be as steep as thatched roofs – where a steep slope was necessary to drain off rainwater.

Another method employing the use of timber was weatherboarding. This is particularly to be seen near the Essex coast and in villages in Kent. The construction is similar to that of the clinker built wooden boats commonly used before plywood, fibreglass and plastic took over. Basic weatherboarded homes do tend to look rather like sheds or beach huts. However, larger, more imaginative versions, where the weatherboarding has been combined with other materials and painted white, can make a much better exterior.

Stone

The areas around London are not completely devoid of stone built houses. Wealthy house owners may have been able to afford to have limestone or even granite transported from other areas but imaginative uses of the occasional rock outcrops have also been made.

Chalk is usually too soft and porous to be used for building but in a few areas a harder chalk (clunch) has been used in conjunction with flint, for example around Petersfield in Hampshire.

Flint is found where chalk is or has been. It formed as nodules in chalk. As vast thicknesses of chalk were weathered away, the flints remained in a deposit called 'clay with flints'. Flints were then collected – often making it easier to farm fields without breaking ploughs – and cemented into walls. This strange nodular rock is used for reinforcing and facing walls in many areas and provides an attractive mottled finish to buildings. Knapped flint has been broken and shaped to produce a flat surface. This smooth, quite shiny, grey/black surface is very weather resistant and can be seen in many walls. Flint faced buildings are often to be found in rural locations as this is the only local stone of many areas around Greater London.

Parts of Buckinghamshire have limestone and this almost white rock is responsible for the name Whitchurch where the church and many houses are constructed from it.

In the same county some villages such as Dinton have houses built of witchert (sometimes called cob). Decayed limestone mixed with clay was combined with chopped straw and water to produce a strong building material, which was built up in layers (called 'berries') into walls topped with thatch or tiles. This was used in the 17th and 18th centuries although it has been used as recently as 1920.

In Hampshire a local stone called Binstead Rock was

used in some properties near Alton including, of course, the village of Binstead.

Parts of Surrey and Kent have outcrops of sandstone south of the North Downs chalk escarpment. Where the sandstone was strong enough to be used, it can be seen in the walls of many houses.

Brick

A substitute for stone is, of course, brick and cement. The clay in many parts of the area provided the raw material for bricks and so our version of the mud hut was constructed. This was done by baking the mud into bricks before putting them together rather than stacking it up and allowing the sun to bake it solid as is the practice in hot, dry and sunny countries.

The chalk of the area provides the basis of cement to fasten it all together and so brick dominates much of our housing, as do tiles for roofing. Roofing materials for brick-built houses may include slate in properties constructed since railway transport became available to bring it from slate producing areas.

The low lying marshy areas provided reeds for thatch and this type of roof is one of the most appealing features of many old brick built properties in the area surrounding Greater London.

Tiles are not only used in roofing but, particularly in Surrey, Kent and Sussex property, they are used to clad brick walls making the familiar tile-hung finish. Many decorative patterns and textures are produced with varied sizes and types of tiles. This makes a distinctive weatherproof finish, comparatively easy to maintain.

Combinations

Fascinating combinations of the above building materials

are often to be seen. This is common where old buildings have been altered and extended over the centuries. For example, brick, flint and thatch made charming country cottages and added variety to the more usual timber and whitewash finish. Brick, stone and slate or tiles are combined in plenty of elegant rural properties built in more recent centuries.

For much of the 20th century, brick, concrete and tiles dominated house construction, resulting in the monotonous appearance of many housing estates. More recently, builders have adopted the varied styles of the past once more. New houses are appearing with weatherboarded, tile-hung and 'timber frame' finishes. These and new brick built houses, are now more likely to adopt styles of the past from the local area. Although these homes are often too close together with only small gardens, they do have some character. They also include more modern amenities than may be found in an original 'period' property.

Older Property

Interesting changes have occurred in the fortunes of older country property. A large proportion of cottages were built for farm workers. With mechanisation of farming, the workforce was cut drastically and there was mass migration to towns and cities.

Before counter-urbanisation started, there was a time, in the last century, when farmers were content to leave old cottages to fall into ruin after redundant workers had left for the city. They did not want strangers living among their fields and there were complicated new rules requiring farmers to improve property to a higher standard if they were to rent it out. When counter-urbanisation got under way, the demand for country property amongst those wishing to escape from London increased and the potential profits made it worthwhile for farmers and other landowners to forget any objections and renovate or sell the cottages for renovation.

More recently, we have heard much about the problems of farming as a business, and there have been pressing reasons to sell buildings for conversion into homes including all manner of barns and outbuildings. In fact, an increasing number of actual farmhouses are being sold to commuters, with a small acreage, while the rest of the land is purchased or rented by a neighbouring expanding farm.

Most of the available farm cottages and buildings around London have now been renovated and converted, providing a great many interesting homes frequently to be seen for sale in estate agents' windows.

For those wishing to do the renovation, the supply has not completely dried up. A trickle of suitable properties still come onto the market, often because they have been occupied until recently by elderly people who could not afford to improve them. The unfortunate fact that retirement/nursing home accommodation often has to be financed by the sale of a house puts properties on the market – some of them in need of renovation. Builders tend to get in first though, so it makes sense to do some fieldwork in the chosen area, asking around at pubs and local shops, whether any such properties are about to come onto the market.

Listed Buildings

These are particularly appealing in a rural setting. The listing process for buildings of architectural and historical importance places obligations on the owners and ensures buildings will not be altered in ways that will damage them and their appearance. At one stage in the not too distant past, it was thought they should be modernised or demolished and rebuilt. In a more enlightened, conservation conscious age, we preserve them. Technology, renovation materials and techniques have been developed to make this possible along with the skills of craftsmen that almost died out but have been rescued, reinstated and once again respected.

As there are substantial penalties for ignoring them, it is most important to go into the responsibilities, rules, and regulations of owning a listed building before even considering the purchase of one. If these are acceptable, a good surveyor experienced in old property and its preservation, should be used. Take care to check that the previous owner has complied with the rules too.

Local council planning offices can usually help establish whether a property is listed and provide the necessary advice on these aspects. Plenty of books have been written on the maintenance and sympathetic improvement of such property.

Build Your Own

Another possibility is to buy a plot of land to have a house built on, or even to do much of the work, if a DIY enthusiast. A problem in our crowded islands is the lack of such available land. Owners are also aware of the shortage, which inflates land prices. Obtaining planning permission with so many rules, regulations and restrictions aimed at conserving the countryside – particularly the Green Belt – is very difficult unless the area has been designated for new housing. Really determined self-build enthusiasts do, however, succeed by being very persistent in their search for a suitable plot. People with large gardens are worth approaching. Unfortunately there are some traps for the unwary.

Some organisations buy a farmer's field and sell it in plots of about one-fifth of an acre. In most cases planning permission is not available and the local authorities can be so much against this process that they apply regulations preventing the plot being used for anything other than agriculture. It may be worth considering investing in such a plot or in any suitable piece of land in the hope of planning permission being gained, as a result of a campaign by plot owners and changes in planning/housing policy applying to the area. *However it is most important to research and be fully informed about the situation concerning possible planning permission before purchase. This includes seeking appropriate professional advice from surveyors, planners and solicitors.*

The government's Land Registry website **http://www.landreg.gov.uk** is useful for finding the owners of potential building plots discovered when visiting an area.

New Developments

Government policy is to build more houses in areas such as the Thames corridor to the east of London and along the M11 route to the north. This increased housing density and coverage may not be to the liking of those who seek the rural scene. Some indications of major proposed and current developments are included in this book but it is not possible to include everything and the situation is very changeable. The attitude of local authorities to this should be investigated along with up-to-date news from local newspapers and local libraries.

On the other hand, if people want to move out of London, there must be more houses built to accommodate them. This was acknowledged with the building of the 'New Towns' beyond the Green Belt in the mid 20th century – such as Basildon and Crawley. These tend not to have great attraction for those seeking the rural idyll. There are, though, many smaller developments including new houses constructed in traditional styles, some of them in new so-called 'Heritage Villages'. Examples are Bolnore to the west of Haywards Heath in Sussex and Great Notley to the south of Braintree, Essex.

There are even some *newly built* thatched cottages. These traditional style homes combine the character of a country home and modern facilities without the problems of an old listed building. They are also less likely to spoil the appearance of an old traditional village if sympathetically planned and constructed.

Employment

Changing Jobs

The possibility of changing to employment out of London – probably at lower than London salaries – needs to be compared carefully with the costs or benefits of remaining in your existing city-based job and commuting. Sometimes it is possible to cope with this change, particularly if mortgage payments are lower on a cheaper property out of London.

Self-employment is tempting, but delay moving home until you have this very carefully planned, researched and established. There are far too many misleading, so called 'business opportunities' and 'home working schemes' advertised in shop windows and even in some 'opportunity' or 'franchise' sections of reputable newspapers. Many of these are attempts to sell manuals on how to start a doubtful enterprise rather than true opportunities. Trading standards offices of local councils can provide advice and warnings about this topic. Above all, do not pay for an 'opportunity' to work at home without checking with the local TSO and/or seeking legal advice.

Commuting

Obviously some travelling will be necessary if a job in London is retained. When commuting is discussed with those involved, the maximum time tolerated is usually quoted as being between one and two hours each way in total. *One hour on trains to a mainline central London station* is taken as the *maximum* for most entries in this guide. This allows for extra time involved in reaching the station and proceeding from the terminus to the place of work. The overall one-way journey should therefore be well within a maximum total of two hours – and often much less – from most locations covered. In fact, most stations in rural areas covered in Part Two are between 25 and 60 minutes from a mainline London station. A few stations mentioned are a little beyond this limit where they serve particularly attractive nearby villages, which deserve to be included.

This definition leads to coverage of the counties that adjoin the boundaries of Greater London and some of the more accessible towns and villages a little further beyond.

Journey durations shown in minutes next to many towns in Part Two, give an *approximate* indication for a typical train journey to a mainline London terminus. This is based on the online timetable for a journey departing between 8 and 8.30 a.m. on a weekday and provides a *rough guide only*. Timetables are often changed so the current situation should be checked when considering the area as a place to live.

The website **http://www.nationalrail.co.uk** can be used to find up-to-date details of times and routes. The terminus indicated is often *one of several alternatives* so it is important to investigate the best route to take. For example, London Bridge may be an alternative to Victoria station and Cannon Street an alternative to Charing Cross. Obviously, do not base a final decision on where to live solely on the approximate journey details provided in Part Two. It is also advisable to try the journey one weekday morning and ask some regular passengers about the current situation concerning the quality of the service.

Telecommuting

An increasing proportion of occupations can be carried out partly from home. Nationally, about one in eight work from home for most or all of each week, and this proportion is expected by many to increase in the next few years. The main increase will be in people working from home for

41

part of the time and travelling to the office for meetings, and so on. This is, of course, being made possible by improved information and communications technology.

Internet access is easily available in all the areas around London. The much faster broadband service is either already available or is being introduced in a rapidly increasing number of rural areas. Campaigns by villagers, with the help of local newspapers and government departments, are increasingly succeeding in getting the required number of expressions of intent to use the service – currently about 250 people – in order to have their local telephone exchange upgraded to the faster capacity.

The government is currently encouraging employers to increase such opportunities. Reducing congestion is a top priority and one reason for this policy decision. As well as the charge for driving into central London, there have been developments to encourage people to work from home and reduce the numbers commuting. The introduction of the UK Government's Flexible Working Regulations (6th April 2002) means that employees are entitled to request to work flexibly if they have a child under the age of six or a disabled child under the age of eighteen, as long as the employee has worked for the organisation for a minimum of 26 weeks. The employer is then obliged to review the request and, if it is possible, to arrange work in a flexible way, arrangements must be made for changes.

Conversely, many employers are realising the benefits of flexible working including working from home. For example, BT has had a very positive attitude towards this and allows several thousand workers to be based at home for much of the time. In other words, consider enquiring about the possibilities.

Education

Moving to a new area can be particularly disturbing for children. They have to leave friends and get used to a new school. Ideally, if possible, the change should be made when the child is about to progress to a new stage in education. On the other hand, the desire for better educational opportunities may be the main reason for a move and this could improve the child's circumstances so much that the benefits of a move overcome any possible disruption and result in a much happier child.

A major consideration in choosing a place to live is the availability of a good education for children and a school in which they will be happy. Unfortunately, the current way schools are organised and the application process seems designed to confuse parents.

Education in the UK has been much criticised over the last two decades. Some justified, some not. A huge number of well-intentioned initiatives have been launched to make improvements and to try to give parents some choice.

There *have* been successes and improvements. However, the opportunities vary widely according to where you live and according to the level of parents' understanding of the system.

The Simple System has Gone

In the past it was quite simple. The local Education Authority allocated children to the nearest school, with few exceptions. Since then, many schools have separated from the local education authority's close control. Others remain closely linked whilst more are somewhere in between.

This change was intended to give schools more control over their budgets and management. Unfortunately, it tends to complicate matters when it comes to applying for school places, as there are different sets of rules and proce-

43

dures. These vary according to how closely linked a school is with its local education authority.

Competition between schools has been encouraged. The more pupils they have, the more money the school gets. Brighter pupils will boost the school's positions in national and local league tables.

Beware the Brochure

State schools now market themselves in a similar way to independent (private) schools.

It is good that much more information is now available. BUT the glossy brochure, or prospectus, will obviously emphasise the best aspects. Some schools which look (from their brochures) successful and ideal are, in fact, "In Special Measures". This means that school inspectors had found so many shortcomings in the schools that they were threatened with closure unless they improved. Fortunately such schools are rare but need to be identified. Some parents may want to support such schools and encourage improvement. However, others may not have such a noble attitude and prefer to apply to the best possible school.

OFSTED Inspection Reports and League Tables

There are many criteria that can be used to compare schools but for secondary schools the most used is the percentage of pupils gaining five or more GCSE grades A to C at the school compared with the average for the area and the UK. For primary schools the performance in SATs tests are often used. These are tests in Mathematics, English and Science. They need to be considered along with OFSTED inspection reports. Above all, it is most important to visit schools, by appointment, while teaching is taking place, to form your own opinion. There is much more to a school than statistics and the comments of inspectors based on their brief visits to a school.

Applications

The procedure for applications to schools varies according to the school.

The advice from the education authorities and schools is, in most areas:

1. Decide where you want to live, bearing in mind the school(s) you would most like to apply to.

2. Exchange contracts for a house near to the school (or take a 12 month rental agreement) so that you can prove you will live near the school.

3. Apply early for a place at the school. Parents do not have the right to choose a school and automatically expect to be given a place there. Obviously the school can take only the number of children it can physically accommodate and there are rules about maximum class sizes.

Parents are usually invited by the local education authority to 'express a preference' rather than make a choice. For schools not administered by the LEA, applications are made directly to the school. In all cases the governors of the school will have established a policy for admissions usually with reference to the LEA's overall policy. This usually gives first opportunity to children already living near to the school and those with siblings already attending the school. After these, those from further afield and new arrivals (e.g. from London) can be considered for places.

4. If a place is not available at your preferred school, a place

is offered elsewhere at the nearest school with a place available. Free transport to the school is usually provided if the journey is more than three miles (two miles for a primary school). This policy is currently under consideration and may change.

5. If you are not happy with this offer, it is possible to appeal. The success of an appeal depends partly on how the appeal is worded and the reasons given. It may be that a waiting list will be used for places that become available at a popular school. The position on the list may be influenced by the outcome of an appeal. In the meantime, the child will attend the school allocated by the LEA.

In the case of some schools such as grammar schools and church schools it may be possible to gain a place without living near the school. Selection tests results and/or regular church attendance are likely to be significant in the admissions policies of such schools. However, it is important to enquire whether transport costs are covered if the journey is over three miles because LEAs are increasingly taking the attitude that children should attend their nearest school when considering this aspect.

The term 'catchment area' is rather misleading. The area is not necessarily fixed but can vary from year to year. The school's admissions policy and decisions made by the head and/or LEA will have more influence than a line drawn on a map. Generally, the nearer a child lives to a primary or comprehensive school, the better the chance of gaining a place at that school although there can be exceptions.

Contacting Schools

Parents are often accustomed to speaking to the Head Teacher at a primary school and smaller secondary schools. However, most secondary schools are much larger and it may not be possible to talk to the Head. The usual arrangement is for the Head to allocate responsibility for dealing with applications and admissions to a particular member of staff. This is often the pastoral Head of Year for the appropriate year group. Do not be offended if the school secretary refers you to this teacher instead of the Head. The person responsible for applications and admissions will be in a particularly good position to help you.

Another point to bear in mind is that this person will also be teaching for part of each day and may have to phone you back. You could also ask the school secretary what time of day would be best for you to telephone again.

Induction

When a place has been offered and you have accepted, most schools provide plenty of helpful information. If there are opportunities to visit the school for particular events it is a good idea to try to do so. It makes the transfer to a new school easier if the child has had a chance to become familiar with some aspects of the school.

Primary Schools

It tends to be easier to find successful and suitable primary schools than secondary schools, because there are so many more of them, giving the possibility of more choice.

Secondary Schools

The majority are comprehensive schools. Much is said and written about remaining grammar schools but there are very few in most areas with the exception of the county of Kent and a few districts of other counties such as Buckinghamshire. Parents are sometimes given the impression by the media that it is worth moving to be within the 'catchment area' of a grammar school.

It is most important to remember grammar schools have selection procedures. Only the top performers in a selection ('11+') test ranking order will gain the places. Gaining a particular mark in the test does not necessarily guarantee a place. Furthermore, each school has its admissions policy set by the school governors. This often allows children from areas well beyond the local, so-called 'catchment' to take the test and compete on an equal basis with local children. The latest, up-to-date situation concerning these matters need to be investigated before allowing the presence of a grammar school to influence choice of location.

Independent Schools (Private, fee charging schools)

These often have smaller teaching groups, making more individual attention possible. Even so, they are not automatically better than all state schools – as is clear from the league tables produced every year. It is particularly important to be provided with as much information as possible. Independent schools have not, until very recently, been inspected in the same detail as state schools.

From Nursery to University

Changes continue across the whole range of education.

The good news: Nursery schools are increasing.

The not-so-good news: They often have waiting lists.

Extra facilities (e.g. advanced computer rooms) are being given to some schools that bid successfully for them.

The good news: Many schools are being given special

status as technology colleges, drama and music schools, and so forth, and money to develop these aspects.

The not-so-good news: These schools with extra facilities are not accessible in all areas equally.

Universities have multiplied at an amazing rate.

The good news: It is intended that half or more of all young people will gain a degree in the future.

The not-so-good news: It is necessary to establish whether newer ones provide more suitable courses than the older traditional universities.

Information on Particular Schools around London

Some indication about schools is included in each chapter about counties as counties have control over many aspects of schools.

It is not possible to mention every one of the thousands of schools in the large area covered around London but some particularly worthy of mention are included. These are by no means the only good schools in the areas covered.

Obtaining Assistance with Finding a Suitable School

Although thousands of pounds are paid to solicitors and estate agents to help with a move from London, they do not provide detailed help with finding suitable schools for children in the family. This type of assistance can be had for a fraction of the cost of their services – from an educational consultant. A suitable consultant can help with unbiased information, research the latest situation in a particular area, contact schools and explain the confusing jargon so often used in connection with the process of finding and applying to schools.

Local Amenities

Hospitals

Moving to the countryside is normally associated with a healthier lifestyle less likely to be affected by the pollution, stress, traffic accidents and violent crime, which tend to affect health in urban areas. However, it is reassuring to know that hospitals exist nearby in case they are needed. For this reason, some information on main (general/acute treatment) hospitals is included in the section at the beginning of the information on each county. A town or village near to the county boundary may have a hospital in a neighbouring county, nearer than the ones mentioned.

Bearing in mind the large area covered, it is impossible to give details of every type of hospital and medical facility. The local health authority for the district will be able to advise on doctors and specialists available for treatment of particular conditions. If there is a particular existing medical condition, it is important to gain full information on the location of treatment for this before considering moving to a particular rural area.

Rural Social Life

Rural communities have traditionally had strong community spirit. It is often suggested this has declined as commuters have moved in and are more concerned with maintaining their links with the city. This may have happened in some cases and at some stages in the recent past. However, it seems that most villages now have a flourishing social life for those who wish to enjoy it and have benefited from the involvement of those newcomers who choose to be involved. In particular, a great many are now living longer and active lives well into retirement. Many of these active retired – often early retired – new villagers have the time, energy and resources to organise and promote village life and community spirit.

The church, local school and in particular the village hall, along with cricket and other sports grounds usually provide the focus for a wide range of activities. A great many grants and benefits have been allocated to the building, rebuilding and improvement of village halls in recent years.

Trying to give full, up-to-date details of all the clubs, sports, fetes, activities and events in every village and country town is impossible. Consequently, it has not been attempted in this book as situations change so rapidly and the information could be misleading. It can usually be assumed that there is a flourishing range of activities not far away from most rural locations near London. Noticeboards outside village halls, churches and schools will give the latest information and contact details for the most active local organisations. Whether the activities will suit all age-groups is another matter, but most villages near London are within quite easy reach of towns with all the usual range of entertainment and social life. Plus, of course, central London is still only an hour or less away!

Access to the Countryside

Living in the countryside does not automatically mean there is access to it. Of course, driving or walking along roads and lanes is permitted but fences and hedges often prevent access to fields beside the roads. This can be a major problem where there are few public rights of way along footpaths. The countryside can be seen from the road but is owned by farmers and other landowners. It is no more accessible to the public than the back garden of a house. If visiting an area and hoping to be able to walk into surrounding land, it is most important to check the opportunities to do so.

Areas covered in later chapters have some indication of the accessibility of the nearby countryside but it is important to check this is adequate when visiting the areas.

A range of Ordnance Survey maps at the larger scales show public rights of way. These can be purchased at major bookshops or can be borrowed from main public libraries. The Definitive Map of public rights of way should be available to view or possibly photocopy in the planning office and library of the area of interest.

There are various ways access can be gained.

Common land is usually accessible to local residents and probably to the general public. There may still be ancient rights for nearby residents to collect firewood or graze animals on the land, although there are many rules and regulations restricting the movement of livestock.

Organisations such as **The National Trust** may make their land available for public access free of charge although this is not a right in law.

Country parks are more than just a few fields in most cases and are a major asset including areas of forest, nature trails, lakes for fishing and open spaces for kite flying, informal ball games, etc. They provide access to areas where the public can wander freely and are usually managed by the local authority to make this as accessible and enjoyable as possible. Bear in mind, though, that they may have closing times and the gates of car parks may be locked at dusk or earlier.

Public rights of way along footpaths and bridleways should be signposted by the local authority where they leave a road. They are increasingly also being way-marked along the route with yellow arrows on fence-posts.

Long distance footpaths are recognised routes with a particular name. These are usually clearly signposted and way marked.

Canal towpaths are often rights of way although only on one side of most canals.

Permissive footpaths are private routes where the landowner has kindly allowed public access but has not made it a right of way. These are usually clearly signposted and may be closed for a day each year to ensure the route does not become a right of way.

The sea wall is mostly accessed by public footpaths.

Beaches and coastal areas washed by the tide are mostly accessible although a right of way is needed to reach it initially. There can be restrictions in some areas of coast.

Trespass is to be avoided but trespass by accidentally leaving a right of way is unlikely to lead to prosecution unless damage has been caused.

If rights of way are obstructed or ploughed up, the landowner should restore them as soon as possible.

Additional Access

A way of gaining access to particular areas not normally available to the public is through membership of organisations that control particular areas of countryside. E.g:

- County wildlife trusts that have nature reserves open to members

- Annual membership of The National Trust and/or English Heritage (for access to the grounds of stately homes etc., without further charge in addition to the annual membership fee)

- Golf clubs

- Angling clubs

- Sailing and boating clubs

Viewpoints

One of the most enjoyable aspects of country living are the scenic rural views. Hedges have been removed in many areas to make larger fields, which are more efficient to farm. This may have the disadvantage of removing a landscape feature and wildlife habitat but has the advantage of making it easier to see the landscape from a road.

The sections on particular areas in Part Two of this book indicate villages with good views from nearby hills. Often it is possible, in hilly areas, to find property with a good view. This can mean exposure to winds and weather, but the view is often sufficient compensation for this.

A combination of good footpath access and interesting views over the rural scene may be important reasons for moving to the countryside.

Points to Consider

Neighbours

It is not usually possible to choose your neighbours. However, a rural area is likely to provide far more opportunities to put space between you and the next building than overcrowded urban environments. Research is also advisable. Hiring a private detective may be rather extreme but some commonsense investigations can be carried out.

Once some localities have been short-listed, try to visit them at different times of the day. It may be worth spending a few days staying in nearby bed and breakfast accommodation. The owners of such establishments are usually mines of local information such as the quality of local schools and the reputations of families living in particular properties. It is worth overcoming any embarrassment connected with enquiries that may seem like 'snooping' – after all, you are about to make one of the biggest decisions of your life. The village gossip is a less reliable source and could be misleading if a grudge is harboured!

A stroll past the properties of interest can provide much information. It may even be possible to get into conversation with nearby residents who may be gardening. Sometimes public footpaths run past the rear of properties and clues such as garden swings, workshops and dog kennels may be seen...

Large-scale maps and aerial photographs are often available from various sources such as local libraries, the Multimap website **http://www.multimap.com** and newspaper offices. These can be useful to pinpoint unexpected aspects such as a nearby sewage treatment plant, waste disposal site or facilities for keeping livestock. A larger property may also have a right of way through its land, giving access to parts assumed to be private.

The Government's Land Registry Website **http://www.landreg.gov.uk** is providing increasingly detailed information, to members of the public as well as solicitors, about registered property boundaries, owner-ship, even the price recently paid for particular properties.

Crime is usually much less than in urban areas but local police may be prepared to discuss particular neighbour-hoods or isolated locations from the point of view of the need for security measures. If there is a Neighbourhood Watch Scheme or Farm Watch Scheme, often indicated by stickers in windows, find out who organises it. This person is usually quite knowledgeable about the area. Get into conversations with the post person, newspaper delivery person and milkman by starting a conversation with enquiries about delivery times and so on.

Look at the condition of nearby properties. If they are in good condition this is promising but if not, it does not auto-matically indicate problems. A rather neglected house may well be occupied by quiet, charming people who prefer to spend their income in other ways. A smart house may accommodate noisy youngsters. This is where walking past at different times of the day can be revealing but with-out being so obvious as to be arrested for loitering with intent!

On a visit to the local authority's planning office, it is usually possible to request details of recent planning appli-cations, whether approved or not. This can give a good idea of the intentions and circumstances of residents in the local area. For example, knowledge of new houses being planned in a neighbour's large garden may influence a decision on purchase of a property before paying a solicitor to discover the same information.

Noise Nuisance

Noise in the country should be less than in urban areas but do not expect complete silence. Remember, arable farmers make their living by using machinery in fields and live-stock do not respect the right of humans to have a quiet lie-in at the weekend. However, noise is likely to be occasional and seasonal, rather than a continuous problem as in urban areas.

Existing rural dwellers often comment that newcomers from cities are not sufficiently tolerant of the inevitable disturbances associated with livestock and farming activities. Wildlife is charming and interesting but does not respect a curfew! As well as hooting, owls may investigate your roof and foxes can be noisy in the mating season. Noise from *urbanised* wild animals, though, is becoming an increasing disturbance in urban areas along with all the usual human hubbub.

Property in rural locations should provide more space for your money so the consequent greater distance from neighbours ought to help provide more peace and privacy than most parts of Greater London. A point worth bearing in mind is that even the most remote and peaceful areas elsewhere in Britain tend to be chosen for low-level flying exercises by screeching air force jets – partly because there are fewer people there to be disturbed! This loud and startling noise nuisance is much less likely to be a disturbance in the more populated rural and semi-rural areas within reach of London: unless you choose to live near an air force base or airport.

Flood Risk

Most rivers have a flat area beside them known as the flood plain. The flat plain is easy to build on but the word *flood* has often been ignored by builders. More and more buildings, roads and other well-drained, waterproof, impermeable surfaces cover or replace the soil. Rainwater is rushed into the river much more rapidly than when it previously, slowly, infiltrated into the soil and took its time to reach the river. The artificial rapid runoff through drains causes rivers to rise much more rapidly in response to rainfall. In other words, buildings on flood plains are not only at risk of flooding but more buildings in the drainage basin of a river increase the frequency and severity of flooding.

Global warming and climate change appear to be causing more rainfall over shorter periods of time. This has increased the frequency of flooding – particularly in recent winters. The authorities are certainly making efforts to improve flood protection but these are often concentrated on the protection of towns. A few rural areas may actually be *adversely* affected if part of the flood protection scheme encourages floodwater to occupy rural flood plains as a 'safety valve' in order to reduce the rush of water into towns downstream.

Likewise on the coast, the very high cost of flood protection against rising sea level and defences against erosion, result in expenditure being concentrated mainly on the highly populated areas. In fact, the policy of 'Managed Retreat' adopted on some stretches of the coast, actually allows the sea to flood and/or erode some lengths of coastline that were previously protected.

The local council planning office should also be able to advise on any risk of flooding if near a river or in a low-lying area near the coast. If there is a risk and the property is still of interest, check with insurance companies exactly the cost of house and contents cover. Sometimes new flood defences have been constructed, reducing risks. Do not assume this influences the availability of insurance cover or automatically reduces premiums. Check that the insurance companies are aware of the improved situation and will allow for it.

In rural areas around London there are plenty of properties in idyllic rural locations above the flood plains of rivers. These may still provide the desired view of the river and its valley but without the risks.

Part Two:

The Counties

ESSEX

Talk of brash, loud and arrogant 'Essex girls' (and guys) irritates the vast majority of Essex residents. It must be obvious to most that no county can be labelled with this type of slander, as there will be a wide variety of characters wherever one goes in the well-populated counties around London.

Inevitably there are a *proportion* of people in Essex who may lack some of the more desirable characteristics as neighbours but these are particularly rare in the more attractive and rural parts of the county. The research recommended earlier in this book will help to reveal the location of any problems near to a property that may be of interest.

There are definite contrasts between the south of Essex near to London and the more rural areas in the middle and north of the county. The Thames attracts industry such as the vast Ford motor works, leading to dense urban areas with many council estates and vast developments of terraced and semi-detached houses. Many of these areas have been smartened in recent years as increased owner-occupancy encouraged improvement – but it can be difficult to escape the urban surroundings, which are really an extension of London.

The government seems intent on extending and intensifying the built-up areas with plans for many more homes to be built in the 'Thames corridor', and the future effects of this are something to investigate if considering this area. It may provide more affordable housing for first-time purchasers but these houses and flats are unlikely to be the type sought by those trying to escape from cramped urban surroundings.

The Green Belt varies greatly in width here, with hardly any Green Belt in evidence at all where the M25 runs between Romford and Brentwood. However, there is Epping Forest and much open countryside to the north-west of Brentwood. This town marks the start of the more attractive areas along the A12 route out of London, into the middle and northern parts of the county.

Much of the south coast of Essex is flat and influenced by the proximity of London and the Thames. However, on approaching the corner from the Thames estuary to the east coast, there are low cliffs and some attractive property overlooking the estuary around Leigh-on-Sea and Westcliff. Some other areas inland overlook woodland and are not far from the coast. Southend-on-Sea is a Unitary Authority largely separated from administration by Essex County Council. The Southend conurbation includes a large built-up area but further north some villages and small towns near Maldon have plenty of suitable property worth investigating.

As most of Essex gives access to road and rail links within an hour of London, the seeker of a more rural residence will probably prefer to head for the varied countryside from Maldon across to Epping and to the north of that area.

Unfortunately, there is a problem to the west: expansion of Stansted Airport. A number of otherwise attractive villages suffer noise nuisance from the rapidly increasing number of flights. In addition, there are plans for large areas of new housing of the type already to be seen to the west of Great Dunmow. The Uttlesford council area has been named as one of the best areas in the country in which to live but it is important to be aware of the present and future effects of the airport, which may eventually reach the size of Heathrow, despite all the local campaigns against expansion. Positive aspects are the availability of more employment, some (overdue) road improvements and the convenience of a nearby international airport for frequent travellers.

Returning to the east coast of Essex, there is the appeal of seaside locations – particularly for families with young children and boating enthusiasts. The two interests may not always combine, though, as although the estuaries are excellent for sailing, they do not always have suitable bathing beaches. The more sheltered estuary areas have most of their sand and shingle covered in thick mud from river deposits. Exceptions are Clacton-on-Sea, Frinton-on-Sea, Walton-on-the-Naze and surrounding area along with much of the coast at Brightlingsea and Southend-on-Sea. These resort towns grew because their bathing beaches are swept clear of mud by waves from the North Sea. Although not, nowadays, destinations for the main annual holiday, they still attract day-trippers and weekenders in large numbers. This makes for a lively atmosphere but also congests the roads in fine weather.

The sea wall footpath provides access to some of the few remaining areas of truly *natural* wilderness in the southern half of England: the salt marshes. These are bleak and bracing areas in winter but breezy and refreshing in summer when the combination of wide skyscapes, colourful sails and the site of huge populations of wild birds are a tonic for those who spend so much time working indoors.

House Prices

Prices in the south-west of Essex are influenced by short commuting times to London but also by the exact area. Former council housing estates have lower prices but are tending to vary according to the amount of improvement carried out by owner-occupants. Unfortunately, some of the 'improvements' may have limited appeal. Other areas, of leafy suburbs, have the larger gardens and garages sought after by families. The price of a semi in the more pleasant areas can be higher than that of a detached home an extra twenty minutes' commuting time out into rural mid Essex.

In the rest of the county the shortage of housing means few areas provide the bargains that have been available in the past. On the other hand, it is still possible to find good value in house size and accommodation in attractive areas – particularly when compared with other counties around London, such as Surrey.

Road improvements such as recently constructed bypasses usually increase property prices because of improved accessibility. Worth bearing in mind, then, are proposed possible developments such as a lower Thames crossing and associated road improvements that may provide an outer route round London. This could possibly run from a new Thames estuary bridge at Canvey Island, northwards along the new A130 dual carriageway. It may then continue via a new road round northern Chelmsford to link with the A120 dual carriageway presently being upgraded across Essex to Stansted airport and the M11. Obviously it is important not to live too close to proposed routes to suffer traffic noise but close enough to benefit from the facility.

Essex Average House Prices

Detached	Semi-detached	Terraced	Flat
280,518	174,723	142,943	114,547

Transport and Commuting

The very busy A roads – particularly the A12 and A127 – encourage rail commuting. The services are frequent and as reliable as in most other areas. The M25 is well known for imitating a car park. Most of the delays are caused by accidents rather than the designs of the roads, which have improved considerably.

Extracts from the 2001 OFSTED Report on Essex Education Authority.

'Essex remains one of the largest LEAs in England. It serves a population of 1.3 million, varying widely in almost all respects. Overall though, the level of advantage in the county is somewhat above average as are levels of attainment of pupils on intake to full-time education. Pupils' attainment at all stages up to GCSE are in line with averages in similar authorities and nationally. Given the context, this points to a measure of under-performance, but the authority has made immense strides in recent years in its school improvement strategy and there are positive signs of improvement in attainment.

'Essex is a large county with a population of about 1.3 million living in urban, new town and rural locations. Its administrative boundaries were redrawn in April 1998 when Southend and Thurrock became unitary authorities. The county has considerable social diversity, including areas of severe disadvantage as well as affluence. Some 37.6 per cent of the population are in social classes one and two, which is higher than the figure for statistical neighbours (36.3 per cent) and for England as a whole (31 per cent). Unemployment in 1999 was above the figure for the South East as a whole but below the national figure.

'The attainment of pupils on entry to full-time education is better than the national average. Pupils' performance throughout primary and secondary schools, up to and including A Level, is mainly in line with that of pupils nationally and in statistical neighbours. Pupils perform above average in Key Stage 3 mathematics tests. At GCSE, the percentages of pupils achieving one A*-G and five A*-C are in line with the national and statistical neighbour averages. The average GCSE points score is above the national figure.'

Additional Notes

The few grammar schools would be expected, of course, to have very good results but outstanding praise has been lavished by inspectors on the grammar schools in Chelmsford and Colchester: they regularly feature in the top ten state schools of national league tables. They are highly selective, taking only the top few percent of the ability range. It is, therefore, unwise to allow these grammar schools to have too much influence on choice of location unless a child is very able. Also bear mind that they are open to applicants who do (extremely) well in the selection ('11+') tests wherever they live. It is possible, then, to live some distance from a grammar school and still be eligible for a place.

Hospitals

Some of the main hospitals include the following:

(Always carefully check the availability of any particular medical services you may require when visiting an area.)

Broomfield hospital, near Chelmsford, is a major hospital already serving a large area of Mid Essex and about to be expanded substantially.

Basildon hospital also serves a large area and is being expanded to accommodate the Essex Heart Surgery Centre.

Harold Wood hospital is just into Greater London near Romford. Surgery is a major activity here. There are plans for it to be replaced with a large new hospital.

Southend Hospital serves a large concentration of population in the south-east of Essex. Parts of the hospital are being substantially modernised.

Colchester General Hospital covers the north east of Essex.

Chelmsford

39 minutes to London Liverpool Street.

The county town of Essex is in the centre of the county. On the map, links with London look good but the station is one of the busiest in the country and the A12 seems to be mentioned on national radio traffic reports more than most other A roads. There are, though, ways round these problems from the more attractive outskirts and outlying villages, such as Writtle, Little Waltham and Great Waltham, Galleywood and Danbury – through the numerous country lanes to other stations nearer to London.

The town centre has benefited from increased pedestrianisation. One side – effect is a surprising number of restaurants, cafes and wine bars with glass fronts like aquariums and some tables outside, possibly in an attempt to give a continental feel. Too many of the old buildings have been demolished or replaced with the standard shopfronts but this may not matter to shoppers more keen on the interiors. The rivers and canal winding through the centre have recently become a centre of more sympathetic development.

Chelmsford has two of the most successful grammar schools in the country: King Edward VI school for boys and Chelmsford County High for girls. This is an advantage only for families with the very brightest children – in the top few percent of the ability range. It is important not to be misled into thinking a move to Chelmsford will automatically secure a grammar school place for a reasonably able child. The schools are open to competing applicants from all over Essex and beyond – via a tough 11+ selection test. Fortunately, the Chelmsford comprehensives have improved to mainly high standards despite having some very able youngsters 'creamed off' to the grammar schools.

The town has grown rapidly with new housing such as the high density Chelmer Village to the north-west and will probably be directed by national government to add more housing estates – most likely to be along the A12 corridor. Plenty of shops in the centre and out of town shopping centres serve the expanding population well.

Chelmsford Average House Prices

Detached	Semi-detached	Terraced	Flat
315,779	184,171	161,502	121,206

Writtle

Writtle is almost joined to Chelmsford but retains its individual character with village green and pond.

Danbury

Danbury is on a hill overlooking rolling and quite varied countryside between Chelmsford and Maldon. This is a large village with views over long distances and good access to walks through beautiful woodland around lakes. Narrow lanes wind down to the Chelmer and Blackwater Navigation – a wide canal with plenty of moorings for pleasure craft and long walks along the towpath as far as the coast at Maldon. National Trust commons provide access to open spaces with rural views. Plenty of varied and interesting houses also have views of these rural attractions.

The busy A414 provides access to Chelmsford and its station. There is also the option of avoiding congested main roads by taking the lanes to other stations along the route to Liverpool Street station.

Little Baddow

Adjoining Danbury is Little Baddow with its up market properties scattered among woodland on the slope down to the Chelmer valley. The secluded and exclusive environment raises property prices above surrounding areas but the London escapee with proceeds from sale of a city property may well find the spacious properties covetable.

Little and Great Waltham

Little Waltham, to the north of Chelmsford, is a quaint and typical country village with a cluster of centuries old buildings around weeping willows and the bridge over the River Chelmer. The flood plain of this river provides peaceful riverside walks through woodland and fields. Property is much in demand here and in nearby Great Waltham with its attractive church and neighbouring picturesque old buildings. The lovely landscape of the Langleys estate has footpaths easily accessible from both villages. Chelmsford station can be reached via several roads. Alternatively, the town can be bypassed along country lanes from the Walthams, to other stations or to the A12, M11 and M25.

Pleshey

Also picturesque – and colourful – when window boxes

and hanging baskets are in bloom, is Pleshey. This village is rather remote, to the north-west of Chelmsford, but is correspondingly peaceful and rural. The attraction of the environment round the old church and remains of the earthworks of Pleshey castle may make the extra driving along pretty country lanes worthwhile.

Boreham and Hatfield Peverel

Boreham and Hatfield Peverel, to the northeast of Chelmsford, are not picturesque but have easy access to the A12 and many properties are within walking distance of Hatfield Peverel station (42 minutes to London Liverpool Street) where it may be possible to gain a seat before the train fills at Chelmsford. Pleasant countryside is not far away to the south, in the valley occupied by the Chelmer and Blackwater Canal on its way to the coast at Maldon.

Little Totham

A quite rare example of a small development of *new* houses designed in the traditional village style, with reasonable sized gardens and open spaces, is 'The Green' at Little Totham advertised by Peverel Estates, specialists in village property.

Maldon

39 minutes via Chelmsford station to London Liverpool Street.

A combination of coast and countryside make Maldon appealing even without direct railway access to London. This small town is well known for its quay with Thames sailing barges and pubs quaint enough to be used in the "Lovejoy" TV series.

Maldon's pleasantly traditional high street includes

interesting shops less likely to be found between Marks and Spencer, Dixon's, and so on, in a larger town. "The Emporium", for example, has an intriguing mixture, including furniture, fabrics, tools, paintings and pet foods. "Victorian evenings", with well-dressed ladies and gentlemen in the high street, make a convincing return to Maldon's past in the weeks before Christmas.

Two large supermarkets and a DIY store are on the outskirts and nearby Chelmsford provides the usual range of chain stores, services and a main-line station for commuting to London.

Schools in the area are above average in most respects. The Plume Comprehensive School in Maldon is one of the largest in the county with over 1,500 pupils. Its size boosts its range of subjects, activities, equipment and sixth form courses beyond that of many schools. Two of the best grammar schools in the country are at nearby Chelmsford. They are very selective and admit only the top few percent of the ability range. This means the comprehensive schools nearby do not suffer the loss of too many able children and can achieve results they are proud of.

Homes overlooking the River Blackwater Estuary, with its boating facilities, are somewhat cheaper than many waterside locations elsewhere. Moorings for boat owners are also far cheaper than on the south coast although thick Maldon mud has to be tolerated (rather than south coast sand) at low tide. This is not a bucket and spade seaside town – because of the mud. For youngsters, though, the large waterside Promenade Park has a seawater paddling pool with a small sandy beach and plenty of playing fields.

Property age and type vary from tiny terraced cottages overlooking the quay, through the regular estates of semis, to unusual houses with rooftop lookout posts giving views for miles. Estates of substantial detached houses have been added in recent years.

Maldon District Average House Prices

Detached	Semi-detached	Terraced	Flat
270,758	156,877	125,741	97,862

Heybridge

A canal from Chelmsford reaches the sea at nearby Heybridge Basin. Very pleasant walks or boating trips along the canal pass a golf course and suitable picnic places. In the Heybridge area of Maldon an expansion has provided many detached houses close to the sea wall, which has recently been raised in response to rising sea levels.

Maldon has a hill – very rare in eastern Essex. Villages to the west of Maldon are in undulating countryside with an unusual abundance of trees – survivors of the subsidised deforestation of the 20th Century. To the east of Maldon "flat and featureless" could apply. But here the villages are surrounded by rows of good value homes. The railway to London is fairly near too, with stations at several points including Burnham-on-Crouch and South Woodham Ferrers.

The eastern villages, in what is known as the "Dengie Peninsula", include some, like Maylandsea, Stone and Bradwell, with access to the sea wall and walks beside one of the most special wilderness areas in Britain: the salt marshes.

Boating and bird watching are main attractions. Many properties here can be described as remote and peaceful. On the other hand there is quite a time-consuming drive along winding country lanes to the nearest stations at Southminster and Burnham-on-Crouch. These are also at the limit of the one-hour train journey to London Liverpool Street.

Bradwell-on-Sea

At Bradwell-on-Sea the ageing nuclear power station no longer justifies its existence – it will stop generating and be partly dismantled – then be preserved while the radioactive core gradually declines over a century or more. Property prices can be a little cheaper in its vicinity... Bradwell is rather small and remote but has a marina with good access for boating in the North Sea and the Essex estuaries.

Bradwell and other villages at the eastern end of the Dengie peninsular involve a rather slow drive through country lanes to reach a station at the edge of the one-hour train commuting range.

Burnham-on-Crouch

Burnham-on-Crouch has better access with its own station a little over an hour to London Liverpool Street (68 mins). The Crouch estuary has water at all states of the tide, helping it to gain status as a major yachting centre. The mud and fast tidal currents make it unsuitable for sea bathing though. Typical Essex weather-boarded buildings combine with Victorian architecture to produce variety in the high street and along the attractive waterfront. The high sea wall cuts off views of the water to some extent but also provides access to long walks along the coast. A big mixture of flats with views of boats, cottages and a variety of semi-detached and detached homes offer varied interest for house-hunters – whether for a main home or second home for weekend boating.

South Woodham Ferrers

54 minutes to London Liverpool Street.

This is a very different type of new town from Basildon and Harlow. It was built for house purchasers rather than those requiring council house accommodation. The emphasis is on the use of traditional materials and styles typical of Essex villages. Steeply sloping roofs and weatherboarding are glimpsed behind the many trees that are now maturing well since they were planted in large numbers along the residential streets during the 1970s and 80s.

Careful planning has resulted in a peaceful environment with Marsh Farm Country Park within easy walking distance and sea wall walks along the narrowing tidal River Crouch. Speed-boats and more relaxing boating activities are sensibly segregated into particular zones on the river.

The town centre has an unusual combination of public library and large, successful comprehensive school in the same building. The other smart traditional style buildings separated from traffic have a good variety of shops plus a supermarket with plenty of free parking. South Woodham Ferrers' own station provides access to London.

Tollesbury

North of the Blackwater Estuary, east of Maldon, is Tollesbury, a village rather remote and not ideal for commuting to London but with a distinctive waterfront of picturesque, preserved, wooden sail lofts, a seawater swimming pool and a well-equipped, carefully hidden marina. A drive through winding lanes and quiet countryside is necessary to reach the mainline to London Liverpool Street at Witham or Chelmsford. The time devoted to this is balanced by the fresh sea air, access to the North Sea and good value housing.

A few properties overlook the marina but the waterfront area has, otherwise, been preserved free of such development. The village itself has a wide range of property types, similar in scope to Maldon.

Colchester

60 minutes to London Liverpool Street.

Following the coast northwards the area comes under the influence of Colchester. The 'chester' indicates a Roman fortification. In fact, this is the oldest town in Britain. There is still a castle at Colchester: a Norman one with Roman foundations. This town is, perhaps, more interesting to explore than others in Essex. The usual chainstores are mixed with small side streets containing a wide variety of buildings and shops of various styles and ages: not just rows of the usual shopfronts.

Colchester District Average House Prices

Detached	Semi-detached	Terraced	Flat
246,513	150,088	126,680	103,832

Colne Engaine

On the outskirts of Colchester a variety of properties provide an interesting choice within reach of open countryside and the coast. The nearby village of Colne Engaine is a popular choice, with its characterful old buildings surrounding the village green.

Wivenhoe, Rowhedge and Fingringhoe

Away from the built-up area of this town and to the south, are attractive waterside villages including Wivenhoe with its train station (just over one hour to London Liverpool Street) and the rather more remote Rowhedge and Fingringhoe. This rather strangely named village has a lovely nature reserve nearby, open to the public.

Mersea

East and West Mersea are on an island. This adds both interest and a slight problem: at high tide the causeway carrying the only access road is often flooded for a short time, cutting the island off from the mainland. A tide table is essential for residents and visitors! A big advantage for boating enthusiasts is access to the sea at any state of the tide via an excellent public pontoon and deep-water moorings nearby. There are also some glorious beaches on parts of Mersea island's coast as well as the inevitable estuarine mud. Unfortunately, it is necessary to drive some distance to a train station (Colchester, one hour to London Liverpool Street) and the tides have to be considered.

Brightlingsea

Rather more substantial beaches and some attractive coastal scenery are to be found on the other side of the River Colne Estuary, in the Brightlingsea area. This is a small coastal town providing a more peaceful setting than the nearby holiday resorts along the North Sea coast at and around Clacton-on-Sea. In this extreme eastern area of Essex we are on the limit of reasonable one-hour train commuting time. There are some pockets of peaceful, attractive countryside in this, the Tendring peninsular, but much is rather monotonous and flat away from the more interesting coastal locations. On the other hand, property prices are lower than most other parts of Essex.

Tendring District Average House Prices

Detached	Semi-detached	Terraced	Flat
178,587	132,850	105,524	95,076

Villages in the River Stour Valley

To the north of Colchester is Constable country. This famous artist revelled in the beautiful landscape of the River Stour valley. Many aspects of his paintings can still be identified in the landscape. The villages, such as Dedham, understandably attract tourists and seekers of property in an area known for its rolling countryside and verdant river scenery. Much is being done to preserve and enhance the attraction of the River Stour. It was fully navigable but its locks now need the restoration being undertaken by The Stour Trust and debates continue over the uses of the river: nature conservation versus full-scale boating activities.

Halstead

Inland and south, away from the River Stour, lays a large and very rural area towards Halstead. This small country town appeals to those who have tired of the city. Its name means 'healthy place' – compared with life in a city. There are plenty of properties of interest in the area – often at prices that may provide plenty of accommodation and space for those selling a London property. The surrounding villages are remote and peaceful but with the railway at

Braintree to provide a link to London.

Braintree

63 minutes to London Liverpool Street.

Braintree is a functional town. Not quaint like some of the villages but purposeful, down-to-earth and charming in parts. The branch line from Braintree links with the main-line to London Liverpool Street station. The fringes of the town have some appealing property and new estates to the east and southwest provide homes not too far from open countryside. Most villages between Braintree and Chelmsford are attractive, such as Terling and the recently bypassed Great Leighs and Little Leighs. Because they have access to particularly pleasant and accessible country-side whilst being near to mainline links and recently improved roads to London, property is much in demand in this area.

Notley

A moderately successful attempt to build a new 'heritage village' is to be found to the south of Braintree at Notley. Some careful planning has incorporated many features of a traditional village although the high housing density may not be to everyone's taste.

Braintree District Average House Prices

Detached	Semi-detached	Terraced	Flat
284,244	158,707	134,343	100,384

Witham

Witham (50 minutes to London) has the advantage of the mainline station to Liverpool Street but has less amenities than many country towns. Although its high street is a conservation area, Witham was chosen to expand in the 1970s with five large housing estates to take 'overspill population' from London. The expansion of housing was not matched by the expansion of facilities for the increasing population. This may not matter if you are prepared to go to Chelmsford or Colchester for a wider range of shops and entertainment.

Wickham Bishops, Great Totham Tiptree

To the east of Witham is Wickham Bishops with plenty of the larger and more individual property in particularly varied and lovely surroundings, often with views over delectable wooded countryside from the hill-top situation. The neighbouring village of Great Totham is similar and some properties may be a little cheaper. Tiptree, to the east of Witham and north of Wickham Bishops, has a wider range of cheaper properties in quite pleasant countryside. Tiptree Heath provides access to peaceful countryside.

Kelvedon and Feering

Moving further out towards Colchester, Kelvedon (51 minutes to London Liverpool Street) has some attractive old buildings. It is popular with those seeking a community with plenty of activities. The rural area around Kelvedon has plenty of open spaces with many large fields full of crops rather than hedges and trees. The neighbouring village of Feering has an appealing and more rural atmosphere: the type of village to have Morris dancers on the village green on May Day.

Coggeshall

To the north of Kelvedon lies Coggeshall. This marvellous, unspoilt, very old village, with its 200 mainly timber-framed listed buildings, has associations with eccentric characters, ghosts and some intriguing scandals. A tourist information leaflet arouses curiosity with: 'Discover sleepy unspoilt Coggeshall, where the ley lines cross and mysterious things happen'. It has been suggested the warrior queen, Boudica, (Boadicea) was buried somewhere in the parish of Coggeshall along with her chariot and jewels.

This intriguing background helps the flourishing trade in the variety of businesses including antique shops in the centre. Interesting speciality shops in superb ancient buildings make for an unusually individual centre to this large village.

Footpaths radiate from the village into varied countryside and include attractive parts of the River Blackwater Valley. Don't be put off by the river's name – the water can be as clear as any other river, until it reaches the muddy estuary! Just outside Coggeshall, to the north, is the Marks Hall Estate with access to the arboretum of interesting trees and unspoilt Essex countryside.

Coggeshall and nearby villages provide a happy hunting ground for residences of character and history as well as the chance of views over the river valley.

The Uttlesford Towns and Villages

(NW Essex – Gt Dunmow to Saffron Walden)

Uttlesford has been voted best place to live in the UK in a recent survey. This can be puzzling as it does not appear as an obvious place on a map, but is the name given to a district – the administrative area of north-west Essex – and is not a town in itself.

This is an agricultural area with some of the best countryside in Essex. An unusually large proportion of timber framed and thatched houses are to be found in particularly attractive small towns and villages. The M11 and improved railway link to London have increased the popularity of this region.

There has been much concern over the impact of Stansted airport expansion which may involve the airport reaching the 1990s size of Heathrow sometime in the not too distant future. But, on the positive side, road improvements such as dual carriageway on the A120, are an advantage of an expanding Stansted airport, which needs better access routes. The expanding airport also provides substantial employment opportunities as alternatives to working in London. New housing development is being encouraged by the government along the western edge of the area – near the M11.

Noise can, of course, be a problem in villages near the airport and under the flight paths. However, predictions of increasing noise nuisance from the airport have to be balanced with the fact that flight paths have been arranged to avoid disturbance as much as possible – and the quieter modern aircraft engines are a big improvement on those of the recent past. More modern, quieter aircraft also have engines which cause less pollution.

Many who travel abroad frequently for business and holidays may tolerate some noise for the convenience of a neighbourhood airport. Furthermore, aircraft noise can be heard in much of Greater London and escapees from London may be prepared to ignore some familiar noise for the substantial other benefits of living in this area. Few locations within reach of the capital experience complete silence.

As with choice of any location it is important to investigate the exact up-to-date situation concerning airport expansion, noise, new road developments and proposed housing estates when considering areas near the airport. Council planning offices and local newspapers should provide the latest information. One of the best ways to assess aircraft noise is to visit the area under consideration during a particularly busy period for holiday charter flights and for the budget airlines which use the airport. However, do not let the airport detract from most of the beautiful rural landscape.

Uttlesford District Average House Prices

Detached	Semi-detached	Terraced	Flat
324,502	209,341	163,093	111,695

Rodings Villages

To the south of the area the Rodings villages are a very popular choice – a line of pretty villages along the River Roding valley. House prices tend to reflect the popularity though. Prices tend to be a little lower further northwards, but are catching up quickly.

Great Dunmow

39 minutes to London Liverpool Street from Chelmsford station.

Dunmow is well known for a strange tradition dating back to 1104. Every four years on a leap year, an award of a flitch of bacon is given to 'whoever does not repent of his marriage nor quarrel, differ or dispute with his wife within a year and a day after the marriage' – Robert Fitzwalter, Lord of the Manor laid down this condition to reward such a happy couple. The celebration of this with a parade and entertaining court of judgement is a major event.

This small, charming and prosperous country town is all within a few minutes walk of open countryside – walks that take you past old and varied buildings, past the attractive pond and along the River Chelmer valley. A little further out is Little Easton with lakes and gardens open to the public.

To the west of Dunmow, towards Stansted airport, areas of housing are under construction near a large supermarket.

Thaxed

To the north of Gt Dunmow lies the architectural gem of Thaxted. A compact concentration of timber-framed buildings – the superb Guildhall in particular – with steep tiled roofs and charming chimneys stand out from the nearby patchwork of arable fields. Overlooking the fields, with an excellent view, is the windmill, restored and housing a fascinating little museum, which should soon be reopened after some recent repairs.

The first weekend after the spring bank holiday is a good time to visit whilst house-hunting – for the sight of 300 Morris dancers processing through Thaxted and dancing until dark.

This is one of the best places to look for the quaint period dwellings often sought after by those tired of modernity in the city.

Saffron Walden

62 minutes to London Liverpool Street from Audley End station.

Saffron Walden is near the north-west boundary of Essex. The yellow crocus used for making saffron is still to be seen in late winter around this outstandingly attractive ancient market town.

A much larger version of Thaxted, Saffron Walden is at the edge of the one-hour train commute to London – by using the nearby Audley End station. On the other hand, there is a better variety of property compared with other places in Uttlesford. As well as being near attractive open countryside, there are many properties overlooking verdant open spaces such as the large green to the east of the town centre.

The local schools are also an attraction for parents and the town is less affected by Stansted airport than others in Uttlesford.

Shopping is a far more interesting experience than in most towns with their carbon copy shopfronts. Explore the shops selling antiques, old books and good quality second-hand goods in amongst the usual modern retail outlets – many of which have been squeezed into carefully preserved listed buildings. Many of these ancient structures have intricate pargetting (moulded plasterwork) decorating exteriors rather than concrete and plastic.

Although most towns and villages have attractive churches, the large and beautiful churches of Thaxted and Saffron Walden are particularly fine.

Finchingfield

This very attractively laid out village must be one of the most photographed in the UK. It frequently appears on calendars and greetings cards. The duckpond surrounded by a village green and picturesque architecture makes this the classic English village. If you walk towards the pond a huge number of ducks and other waterfowl will rush towards you across the green, hopeful of a feeding. A rather low-level church and smart windmill complete the perfect rural settlement scene.

Period houses are plentiful here and in surrounding villages such as Great and Little Sampford. Remoteness may be compensated by the pleasant rural surroundings.

Stansted Mountfitchet

58 minutes to London Liverpool Street.

Stansted has the distinction of being a village with an international airport. However, aircraft noise varies according to exactly where you are in the village and surrounding locality. It tends to affect other villages more than Stansted itself. Locations affected depend on the flight paths being used, flight frequency and timing. These have been designed to try to minimise the impact on as many people as possible: particularly at night. Nevertheless, it is wise to visit the areas under consideration at various times to establish exactly the effects of the airport and to enquire about the likely effects of future expansion plans. More modern aircraft have much quieter engines, which cause less pollution.

An advantage of the developments nearby is the improved access to London. Stansted has its own station and the M11 is not far. These also provide easy access northwards to Cambridge for possible alternatives to working in London.

With airport matters to consider, it is easy to overlook the facts that Stansted is an old settlement with some 400-year-old buildings, a windmill, three tearooms and the remains of a castle, now imaginatively turned into a tourist attraction representing many aspects of the past in a lifelike manner.

To the north of Stansted are many attractive villages. Quendon, Elsenham and Manuden provide a hunting ground for suitable property with quaint cottages and more modern developments at Elsenham. Ugley is not.

Newport

Newport is between Stansted and Saffron Walden. Its station provides London Liverpool Street access just within the one-hour range. It has an eye-catching main street with its line of appealing old buildings. The countryside becomes more hilly here than much of Essex, as the chalk of the Chiltern Hills begins to show through ploughed fields.

Nearby, idyllic country villages of Clavering, Widdington, Arkesden and Rickling Green have cottages scattered around village greens and cricket pitches. Anyone seeking the archetypal thatched cottage should explore this area.

Epping

38 minutes to London Liverpool Street on the Central Line.

Epping is to be seen on underground railway maps (actually *overground* at this point). Commuting is, therefore, easier than from many similarly attractive locations in Essex.

Shops are strung out along the very busy high street. Away from this main road a variety of property types, including many detached houses with views from elevated positions, provide scope for the house-hunter.

Epping Forest District Average House Prices

Detached	Semi-detached	Terraced	Flat
461,928	271,965	209,880	154,250

A main attraction is, of course, nearby Epping Forest. This is one of the largest remaining fragments of ancient forest that once covered most of the area around London. The gnarled old oak trees, ponds, networks of footpaths and bridleways provide magical and peaceful retreats to explore. Being on a hill, frequent stunning views over the Lea valley and London add interest to this very accessible area of countryside. Herds of wild deer roam the forest and move into the surrounding countryside at times. They are difficult to find when walking but can also make unwelcome appearances crossing roads – beware of this and watch your speed!

Chigwell

To the south of the forest, Loughton and Buckhurst Hill are more suburban than rural but Chigwell, sometimes called the first village out of London, is more semi-rural and has many attractive properties close to Green Belt countryside. This was where the TV series *Essex Wives* was based – this may or may not help to recommend the area depending on one's attitude to life!

Waltham Abbey

To the north of Epping Forest the ground drops away to Waltham Abbey, with its small town atmosphere and some spread-out villages with interesting properties.

Roydon

Roydon (40 minutes to London Liverpool Street) stands out as particularly characterful with many listed buildings. Georgian style dominates in parts creating quite formal, rather than quaint, appearance. Footpaths lead to the nearby quite picturesque canal and lanes lead off to the delectable country via many substantial detached properties.

Harlow

38 minutes to London Liverpool Street.

Harlow new town, built in the mid 20th century, provides a huge contrast to Roydon. It was planned to be as self-sufficient as possible, providing varied housing, shops and services and as much local employment as possible so that commuting to London would be unnecessary. It has property cheaper than many surrounding rural places and may appeal to those who like this type of settlement but perhaps not to country lovers. It does provide well-designed access to a large shopping precinct, serving a large surrounding area.

Harlow Mill and Old Town

The nearby Harlow Mill (with its station) and Old Town areas provide more possibilities for finding interesting and varied property, as do the villages to the east. Country houses are particularly appealing in this area with the comparative proximity to London.

Harlow District Average House Prices

Detached	Semi-detached	Terraced	Flat
279,351	181,864	137,830	98,030

Stapleford Abbotts and Havering atte Bower

Stapleford Abbotts and Havering atte Bower are close to the built-up area of Romford (27 minutes to London Liverpool Street) but this area, on the fringe of Greater London, is surprisingly rural – mainly because Green Belt policy preserves the area. To the south-west is the huge sprawl of mainly council estates in Harold Hill. Then the Green Belt narrows to almost nothing where the M25 ploughs through, separating the contrasting town of Brentwood from the dense urban area of Greater London.

Brentwood

38 minutes to London Liverpool Street.

Many move to Brentwood to apply to the very successful comprehensive schools. Here is an example of the comprehensive system working well, and the schools are oversubscribed with applicants from far beyond the area that might be regarded as their normal catchment. These are not to be confused with the independent school near the town centre, which some parents feel may be even better.

The town has a busy and congested but a traditional high street despite the A12 bypassing it. Even so, it has something of the country town atmosphere despite its nearness to the edge of the London conurbation. Away from the centre, though, are plenty of tree-lined avenues with substantial properties giving an air of prosperity – particularly in the Shenfield and Hutton areas. This town has the distinction of figuring particularly highly in the ownership of cars per household – this could be why there is a congestion problem at times! Although substantial employers of office workers such as BT and the Ford Motor Company are based here, the vast majority of the working population commute from stations at Shenfield and Brentwood.

Two large country parks – Weald Park to the north and Thorndon Park to the south, make rolling and wooded countryside easily accessible from most parts of this town. The site of Brentwood is on a hill, giving some properties long distance views over these parks and the Thames valley.

Brentwood District Average House Prices

Detached	Semi-detached	Terraced	Flat
403,887	235,974	186,468	172,071

Chipping Ongar

Chipping Ongar, to the north of Brentwood, retains its traditional charm with its high street narrowing from the former market area to a very small gap between buildings often clipped by passing vehicles. Small independent shops are mixed with the usual range of retailers. Although it was once linked to the underground railway system, commuters now need to go to Epping for the central line or Shenfield (30 minutes to London Liverpool Street) for mainline trains to Liverpool Street station.

The local comprehensive school closed and its land is now redeveloped with new housing. Many local children attend the Brentwood schools such as the highly regarded Brentwood County High School and Shenfield High.

Billericay

Billericay (38 minutes to London Liverpool Street) is smaller but similar in some ways to Brentwood and has some desirable property on the outskirts near Norsey Wood. It is a big contrast to Basildon New Town, only a few miles away.

The area to the south of Brentwood, down the hill to the A127, has the villages of Little Warley and Childerditch, Ingrave and Herongate – quite attractive locations close to London.

Ingatestone

36 minutes to London Liverpool Street.

North of Billericay and Brentwood, along the A12 towards Chelmsford, is Ingatestone (meaning 'settlement at stone'). The 'stone' was dropped there by a melting ice sheet, which had transported it hundreds of miles, during the last ice age. The stone was devil-worshipped, and then broken in three by Christians to break its 'evil influence'. One piece is beside the church. The other two are either side of Fryerning Lane, where the devil is keen for them to scratch as many cars as possible on turning the tight corner from the high street! This narrow Roman Road high street was wide enough for Roman legions to march along, but it is just as well the A12 bypasses this large village. The shops and buildings strung along the high street have a pleasant traditional appeal. There are no concrete pedestrian precincts.

An attraction is the successful Anglo-European school. This was one of the first 'specialist' comprehensive schools. Most secondary schools are now being encouraged to take on a particular speciality. It can be science, music, drama or whatever area the school excels at. In this case it is links with the European Union and languages in particular. A family living some distance from Ingatestone, with links to the E.U., can stand an improved chance of children being accepted after local children have been given places.

Open plan groups of large detached houses such as Willow Green near the Anglo-European school are particularly 'sought after' properties. The countryside is nearby and accessible with peaceful wooded walks towards Fryerning village.

Ingatestone station has a friendly village atmosphere and is more pleasant than many station environments on this line. Unfortunately the trains can become full before they reach here from Chelmsford at busy periods.

Many attractive villages around Ingatestone provide plenty of property choice in rural surroundings all around Ingatestone including Blackmore, Doddinghurst, Mountnessing and Margaretting. One particularly popular but expensive village is Stock.

Grays and Thurrock

South of Brentwood, into the flat former flood plain of the tidal River Thames, are some pockets of countryside but the area down to Grays (38 minutes to London Fenchurch Street) and Thurrock is less attractive for those seeking rural surroundings. Millions of shoppers know the area for its Lakeside shopping centre with plentiful car parking and range of retail outlets, services and entertainment, just off the M25. Property prices are lower here than in more appealing areas further north.

Thurrock Unitary Authority District Average House Prices

Detached	Semi-detached	Terraced	Flat
270,586	166,021	134,112	103,077

Thames Gateway and Thames Chase

The environment of this area is being improved by a group of organisations, local authorities and volunteers establishing a new community forest called Thames Chase. The intention is to 'screen urbanisation in a veil of trees and lush greenery, soften the hard edges of contemporary development and breath new life into tired neglected land'. Progress has been made towards a more varied landscape with forest, open spaces and outdoor leisure facilities. Much more improvement is planned.

On the other hand, it is planned to locate 110,000 new homes in the Thames Gateway area. Hopefully, the intended sustainable environmental improvements will be combined effectively with the proposed new affordable housing. This is an area to watch for the future.

Basildon

37 minutes to London Fenchurch Street.

The new town of Basildon was developed with the intention of being self-sufficient like Harlow, described earlier. It certainly succeeded in accommodating a big proportion of London's 'overspill' population in large council estates. Those who can afford to choose more rural surroundings will not be attracted to this densely built-up environment. Although not intended to house commuters and originally without a station, one was built at a later stage.

Oil refineries do not provide the most appealing view in areas to the south of Basildon but there is some access to the tidal Thames for boating activities.

Basildon Average House Prices

Detached	Semi-detached	Terraced	Flat
266,487	172,469	131,690	90,419

Southend-on-Sea

60 minutes to London Liverpool Street or Fenchurch Street.

This is a large urban area with a big proportion of the Essex population. It is unlikely to suit those seeking the rural idyll – only a few locations on the outskirts of the conurbation such as Hockley (48 minutes to London Liverpool Street) and Daws Heath may provide an appropriate environment. Plenty of substantial properties to the east and west of Southend provide views of the sea and Thames estuary plus some green and pleasant areas preserved on the low cliffs. An example is the (rather small) Hadleigh Country Park.

The town provides all the attractions expected of a major shopping centre and seaside resort. Formerly popular for the annual holiday, it is now still chosen by many from London and elsewhere for days out to enjoy the beach, boating, amusements and the impressively long pier.

Grammar schools here are very selective, as elsewhere in Essex.

Two railway lines link this area to London, providing a choice of route to Liverpool Street or Fenchurch Street stations. Rail travel may be preferable to the congested A13 and A127 roads towards London.

Southend-on-Sea Average House Prices

Detached	Semi-detached	Terraced	Flat
272,701	174,044	139,793	101,038

Castle Point

The district of Castle Point is sandwiched between Basildon and Southend-on-Sea. It includes a variety of mainly urban areas although it is possible to get away into open spaces and woodland in some parts and to get views over the Thames Estuary. Although some comparatively low-priced property is interesting and road and rail links (40 minutes to London Fenchurch Street) are nearby, most of this area cannot be recommended as providing an idyllic rural environment.

Castle Point Average House Prices

Detached	Semi-detached	Terraced	Flat
201,699	162,043	140,704	97,477

Rochford

50 minutes to London Liverpool Street.

To the north of Southend is the Rochford district. This is

much less urbanised and many of the villages here are scattered over the mainly flat countryside. Whether it is flat and boring or a wide-open refreshing area of countryside with appealing skyscapes, is a matter of opinion. The marshes to the east and north, near the coast, are, in many parts, a true natural wilderness. Walks along the sea wall certainly allow one to get away from it all. On the other hand, the remoteness of villages in parts of this district means a long drive along winding lanes to reach a railway station.

The town of Rochford does continue the built-up area from Southend beside the small airport but further north the rural areas open up and to the west the ground rises a little to Hockley, making this location much more attractive.

Rochford District Average House Prices

Detached	Semi-detached	Terraced	Flat
296,136	172,877	144,749	116,567

Hullbridge

47 minutes to London Liverpool Street from Battlesbridge station.

Hullbridge is beside the River Crouch. This is a sprawling arrangement of mainly 20th century housing with access to walks along the sea wall and boating facilities. Extensive views over the tidal river may be possible from some properties here and at South Fambridge.

Battlesbridge

47 minutes to London Liverpool Street.

At the head of navigation on the River Crouch is Battlesbridge with its maltings building converted into an antiques centre surrounded by many units selling a fascinating range of collectables, furniture and bric-a-brac. The railway is nearby and a recently completed dual carriageway route for the A130 helps with access to other areas.

HERTFORDSHIRE

Much of the south and south-west of Hertfordshire is influenced by its proximity to London with large urban areas such as Watford almost becoming an extension of the London conurbation. However, there are great contrasts over short distances. Half of the county's area is Green Belt. Country lanes and quaint villages can be found in pockets of countryside between the thriving modern towns and historic market towns such as St. Albans, Hitchin and Hertford. The towns also provide fast rail links to central London.

There are some attractive woodlands, river valleys and hills. In particular, the chalk Chiltern Hills that run from the west into the north of the county are designated an Area of Outstanding Natural Beauty. Canals, rivers and lakes add to the scenery and opportunities for outdoor activities. Between the motorways and main roads are typical English rural scenes, particularly in the north and east of the county.

Watling Chase Community Forest is 72 square miles overlapping south Hertfordshire and north London around Potters Bar, St Albans, Bushey, Borehamwood and Barnet. As with other community forests set up towards the end of the 20th century, Watling Chase consists of a mixture of public open spaces, farmland, meadows, hedgerows as well as woodland which is being substantially increased. The intention is to regenerate the countryside, improve the environment and make green spaces more accessible in and around nearby urban areas.

Historical aspects give Hertfordshire some identity. The Romans originally chose the present site of St Albans for

Verulamium and built roads to the north. The village of Dane End is a reminder of the county's position as a frontier in the two-century struggle between Saxons and the Danish invaders. There are many mansions such as Hatfield House with strong historical associations. These show the county has always been a popular place to live. The Grand Union Canal was once an important link with the industrial Black Country. After a period of decline caused by the coming of the railways the canal has become a main route for cruisers and narrowboats plus an interesting corridor to the countryside for walkers. Likewise the canalised River Lea.

Another effect of the railways was what Ebenezer Howard called the 'malignant urban sprawl' as commuting to London became possible. This Victorian pioneer planned the 'garden city' including a spacious layout with gardens, park-like setting and cottage-style residential areas. Letchworth was the first to be built in this style followed by Welwyn Garden City early in the 20th century. These were imaginative attempts to provide a pleasant environment in a planned new settlement mainly for residents formerly living in London. The new towns of Stevenage, Hemel Hempstead and Hatfield, built in the mid 20th century, may not be a popular choice for readers of this book. One of the main problems with these towns is the lack of parking space for families now likely to have more than one car.

Much of the UK film industry, along with TV studios, is located in the south-west of Hertfordshire. Much growth has occurred recently, with top directors and screen and TV stars frequently working in Elstree studios and the millennium studios including the Leavesden facilities.

Hertfordshire Average House Prices For The Second Half Of 2003

Detached	Semi-detached	Terraced	Flat
413,056	237,449	183,551	137,965

Schools

Hertfordshire has the benefit of schools and education system largely praised by OFSTED inspections. Standards achieved by children are generally higher than national averages. Low unemployment and a mainly well educated and quite prosperous adult population helps.

Extracts from the 2000 OFSTED Report on the LEA:

'The proportion of adults with higher education qualifications is above the national average: 17.6 per cent compared with 13.5 per cent. The proportion of pupils eligible for free school meals is smaller than the national average: 10.3 per cent in primary compared with the national average of 19.9 per cent; seven per cent in secondary schools compared with the national average of 17.5 per cent.

Hertfordshire baseline assessment data shows that pupils' attainment on entry to primary schools is above average; attainment at the end of Key Stages 1, 2 and 3 in English and mathematics is above national averages.

The proportion of pupils achieving five or more GCSE A*-C grade passes is above the national average. The proportion of those achieving at least one A*-G is in line with the national average.

The proportion of pupils attaining GCE A level or

Advanced GNVQ certificates in two or more subjects is in line with the national average.

Standards are rising in Hertfordshire schools faster than the national rates.

Some schools with similar characteristics have differing levels of achievement.

The quality of teaching in primary schools is in line with national figures.'

Additional notes

The mainly comprehensive system includes plenty of good, successful schools and some that have selection procedures. Grammar schools in Watford are substantially oversubscribed and it is important to remember only children with high academic abilities stand a chance of gaining a place. There is less risk of being allocated to a school 'in special measures' or 'achieving improvement' in this county than in many others. Towns with high-achieving comprehensive schools include Harpenden, Bishop's Stortford, St Albans, Hitchin, Potters Bar, Hemel Hempstead, Hitchin, Wewyn Garden City and Sawbridgeworth.

Hospitals

Some of the main hospitals include the following:

(Always check the availability of any particular medical needs carefully when visiting an area.)

Queen Elizabeth Hospital in Welwyn Garden City serves much of the eastern side of the county. The hospital has had many parts upgraded and refurbished recently.

The Lister Hospital, Stevenage serves the area around this town.

Chase Farm Hospital, Enfield is a long established hospital which has had substantial upgrading recently.

Hemel Hempstead Hospital is smaller than those above but is developing a special facility for treating the sudden onset of chest pain and heart disease.

Watford General Hospital serves southwest Hertfordshire. Its A&E department has recently been refurbished and enhanced.

East Hertfordshire

East Hertfordshire Average House Prices

Detached	Semi-detached	Terraced	Flat
381,771	237,694	184,635	139,118

Bishop's Stortford

47 minutes to London Liverpool Street.

The town centre is typical of a small old rural market town. Over the last twenty years the town has doubled in size, with four housing developments on the edges of the original town. Even so, it has largely retained its rural atmosphere.

The north-west area of the town has many large houses and leafy surroundings. Some attractive property is on the east side, within quite easy reach of the station. One of the new developments, St Michael's Mead, includes Georgian style houses around an elegant square.

Points to bear in mind are that Stansted airport is five miles away and the government currently proposes to encourage the building of 200,000 houses on the M11 London to Cambridge corridor. The expanding airport provides increasing employment opportunities without travelling to London. While the proposed house-building will provide more homes from which to choose, they will, of course, cover parts of the countryside which is an attraction at present.

Standon

Standon is west of Bishop's Stortford. It has a curving, wide high street because it was once a market town. Timber framed 16th century houses are an attraction here.

Much Hadham

A few miles to the west of Bishop's Stortford is Much Hadham, one of the oldest and most picturesque villages in Hertfordshire. 16th and 17th century cottages are abundant here in a smart and prosperous environment boosted by historical connections with the Bishop of London. The village is in the valley of the River Ash and had a smithy, now part of a crafts museum. There is very good access to the attractive countryside along footpaths and bridleways. Bluebell woods on the east side of the river are particularly lovely as an area to get away from it all.

The Pelhams

To the north of Much Hadham are a group of villages with the name Pelham. These villages are on a low level plateau dissected by streams to make quite verdant rolling countryside. Many hedgerows have been removed here as in most country areas where there were incentives for farmers to produce as much grain as possible during the latter part of the 20th century. However, some mixed woodlands help to add interest to views over the fields. The scattered mixtures of properties are constructed of timber frame, thatch, brick and tiles. Be aware of the River Ash. It looks small and insignificant most of the time but can swell greatly to flood Violets Lane and other parts of its flood plain.

Stocking Pelham is particularly pretty. The number of pylons and cables to the east of the village spoil some views but are gradually being hidden by trees.

Westmill

Westmill is nearby and well known as a winner of the national "Best Kept Village" competition. This is certainly an excellent example of an English village said to have been particularly appreciated by Queen Victoria. The River Rib runs through the recreation ground surrounded by trees, making a very scenic route for a stroll in idyllic surroundings. A cricket field brings the sound of ball against bat to the otherwise peaceful surroundings of the 11th century Church of St Mary. A charming mixture of cottages and houses include lath and plaster, flint, weatherboard and brick plus some fine Georgian houses.

Benington

Benington, arranged around a typical village green and duck pond, is to the west of Bishops Stortford, towards Stevenage. Quaint timbered cottages are clustered around the green providing mouth-watering possibilities for cottage-hunters. The Georgian house, Benington Lordship, has superb gardens, open to the public. The gardens incorporate the ruins of a Norman castle next to the medieval church.

Buntingford

On the Roman road, Ermine Street, now the A10 Cambridge to London route, Buntingford is a small country market town, centred around a long, straight and narrow high street. Plenty of smart Georgian and timber framed buildings are strung out along this street including small traditional shops, historic pubs and restaurants. A riverside footpath, called 'Pigs Nose', leads to Layston Court Gardens cared for by the Town Council.

Sawbridgeworth

55 minutes to London Liverpool Street.

The small town of Sawbridgeworth has retained its historic character. Set in the east of Hertfordshire, on the banks of the River Stort, it is close to a line of woods and fields that follow the valley of this river. Riverside walks and in summer, motorboat cruises on the River Stort provide access to tranquil countryside.

A well-known fruit tree nursery established by John Rivers flourished here for over 250 years. Many modern houses have the former nursery's fruit trees in their gardens. In recent years, Sawbridgeworth's riverside maltings have been converted into an antiques centre, small business units and many homes with views over the river valley.

A blend of past and present with steep tiled roofs and overhanging timber-framed upper storeys, provides a calming atmosphere. The Market Square and Fair Green have a village pump, attractive old houses and quaint old shops. Among newer property are the flats overlooking the navigable river here. The station has fast connections with London Liverpool Street and the opportunity to take to country roads avoiding congestion.

Stanstead Abbotts

To the west of Sawbridgeworth is Stanstead Abbotts, which should not be confused with Stansted Mountfitchet. The other Stansted – without the 'a' – is the one with the airport.

Riverside walks can be enjoyed here and the marina, with its colourful narrowboats and cruisers, provides facilities for boating enthusiasts. In one direction along the River Lea is open countryside and the River Stort and in the other, boating access to London's canals which, in turn, link with the River Thames and the whole canal network. Commuting by canal is too slow but has possibilities for boat owners with liveaboard accommodation – for workdays on a London mooring!

The large village of Stanstead Abbotts is at the northern end of the Lea Valley Park, which provides good access to open spaces, rivers and lakes along the valley. This location is also close to London and has fast rail links for commuting.

Ware

40 minutes to London Liverpool Street.

This market town has a mixture of ancient and modern streets on the end of the arm of urban development that extends along the Lea valley northwards from London. In fact, there is open countryside almost surrounding this unspoilt settlement. It has the designation of "outstanding archaeological and historical interest".

Behind the high street shops are some old stables converted into mews houses. The industrial archaeology is also likely to be of interest to escapees from London – the old maltings near the river have been converted into flats with views of passing narrowboats and access to magical walks along the river. Beautiful gardens, decorated with old gazebos, line the river before you reach open country-side.

Ware still has industry but most of it is not the ugly, intrusive type.

The long and quite picturesque high street has the major retailers plus smaller specialist shops and a variety of restaurants.

Great Amwell

Great Amwell village, to the south of Ware, is a pretty and popular village for those able to afford the property prices inflated by celebrities who have chosen this attractive area. Emma's Well, which probably led to the name of this village, is in the grounds of Well House with colourful gardens extending down to the road.

In 1609 Sir Hugh Middleton started to excavate the New River to take water from Chadwell Spring to supply London. Near to Emma's Well the river widens to make a pool with two islands. Concerts are held here with floodlit water and trees making an atmospheric backdrop to the performances.

Hertford

44 minutes to London Liverpool Street.

Hertford has the distinction of being the County Town of Hertfordshire although certainly not the largest town in the county.

Parts of this market town may be too urban for those seeking a country home but it provides a decent town centre for shopping and eating out.

Hertford castle is surrounded by a haven of tranquil riverside gardens. In fact, four rivers meet in the town and give access along paths to Folly Island with its 19th century cottages and Hartham Common, ideal for walks, picnics and sport. Riverside walks and cycle paths also lead out into the country and on to Ware among other destinations.

Two stations provide access to London King's Cross or Liverpool Street.

High Molewood, Great Molewood and Bengeo

In the High Molewood and Great Molewood areas of north Hertford, chalet bungalows and good-sized detached houses are located on private unmade roads in a pleasant woodland environment. The Bengeo area is a smart suburb and on the south side of town are a considerable number of large Edwardian and Victorian houses.

Stevenage

29 minutes to London Kings Cross.

This New Town is unlikely to provide the environment sought by readers of this book but the train journey from here to King's Cross is fast and frequent. A large traffic-free shopping centre is the main attraction.

Stevenage Old Town was the original Saxon settlement. This has more interesting possibilities, with its conservation area of covetable village buildings.

North Hertfordshire

North Hertfordshire Average House Prices

Detached	Semi-detached	Terraced	Flat
321,487	206,153	156,864	119,409

Royston

46 minutes to London Kings Cross.

Royston is located at the foot of the Chiltern Hills in the far north-east of the county. The ancient roads known as the Icknield Way, from Cornwall to Great Yarmouth and Ermine Street, from London to the north of the Roman empire, cross at this point making an obvious, accessible point for a market town. Main roads and railway still make this town accessible and suitable for commuting to London or Cambridge with plenty of alternative country road routes if there are traffic congestion problems.

Upper King Street has many interesting old buildings but the town is really a modern community with shops and services serving the surrounding area. An advantage for parents looking for homes near schools is the access to two education authorities: Cambridgeshire as well as Hertfordshire.

Rather high-density housing estates, particularly in the north of the town, may not be particularly appealing. The larger Edwardian and Victorian homes within reach of nearby heath and hills may be more interesting.

Barkway

Plenty of villages surround Royston. Barkway, to the south, has many attractive Georgian and timber-framed houses. This village is on the eastern edge of the Chiltern Hills. These, and Periwinkle Hill, give good views over the plains of Cambridgeshire.

Nearby Barley is a comparatively basic village but with footpaths providing interesting walks through rolling countryside.

Therfield

Therfield is south of Royston and is particularly interesting with many old houses from the 16th, 17th and 18th centuries. It lies on the ridge of the Chilterns where there are historic long barrows – earthworks dating from the Iron Age. Therfield Heath provides access to open countryside. Its name means 'dry land' on well-drained chalk slopes. This village has won the title of Best Kept Village in Hertfordshire many times.

Kelshall

Kelshall is 550 feet up in the Chilterns, often referred to as the East Anglian Heights in this area. Good views can be enjoyed from the surrounding countryside. The altitude means snow is more common here than in some lower areas. This gives a new, charming appeal to the views at times in winter, but can be a problem for drivers on a few of the coldest days.

Sandon

Also on the chalk ridge is Sandon. Just behind the buttressed 14th century church is a good viewpoint, which looks down on fields and the scattered houses.

The permeable chalk here is dry but in this area early settlers found a good water supply in ponds. These had formed in hollows in the impermeable boulder clay, which occurs in places on top of the chalk.

Baldock

46 minutes to London Kings Cross.

Baldock is a small and traditional market town with olde-worlde charm. Its history as a stopping place for horse-drawn coach transport, means plenty of pubs and restaurants are to be found in its wide high street. Despite competition from a large Tesco superstore, the shops in the centre of Baldock still flourish on the products and services not supplied by the large competitor.

This town has some appeal for those seeking to get away from the concrete jungle of larger built-up areas. It has a convivial environment, with a good choice of Victorian, Georgian and timber framed houses. Many streets are tree-lined – even in the more modern areas.

The local comprehensive school is successful and popular.

The railway and A1(M) is nearby. This route tends to be very congested at peak times but from the Baldock area there are alternative country roads worth a try.

Access to the countryside is rather limited by Letchworth, close by to the west, but there is a pleasant hilly area to the east, with views from Windmill Hill.

Ashwell

To the north of Baldock, Ashwell is a particularly outstanding example of an attractive Hertfordshire village. All villages have a church but Ashwell's is particularly noticeable with its highly ornate tower, rising to 176 feet and crowned with an unusual octagonal lantern. A delightful variety and large number of interesting properties include medieval cottages, plastered or timbered, thatched and tiled town houses and the Maltings, now converted into flats. The attractiveness of this village raises its house prices in comparison with other locations in North Hertfordshire.

Wallington

Wallington is to the east of Baldock among woodlands and with plenty of footpaths giving access to peaceful countryside. Some interesting barns are located next to rolling farmland.

Rushden

Midway between Baldock and Buntingford, Rushden is on a high plateau behind the nearby chalk ridge. The buildings are scattered in an appealing layout. The surrounding hamlets of Southern Green, Shaw Green and Cumberlow Green have a number of properties with good views of open spaces and include 17th century houses and cottages.

Weston

Weston lies on top of a hill south of Baldock and has plenty of interesting buildings including the brick-built 19th century windmill. Some new housing has been inserted in gaps in a reasonably sympathetic way. Plenty of footpaths give access to views from the hill. One gravel footpath, across the village green, was made for the Manor butler to get from his home to the Manor House without getting his feet wet and muddy.

Graveley

Graveley is to the south of Baldock and just north of Stevenage – perhaps uncomfortably close to this spreading New Town. One of the special features of this village is its pond, originally the main source of water for those who did not have their own well. Many houses here are very old although their timber frames have, in some cases, been covered with pebbledash and Georgian brick fronts.

Letchworth

36 minutes to London Kings Cross.

This is the world's first Garden City, founded in 1903 and planned by the Quaker, Ebeneezer Howard. This Victorian pioneer planned the original 'garden city' including a spacious layout with gardens, park-like layout and cottage-style residential areas. This introduced new ideas in planned development and innovative design and still attracts visitors from all over the world to see and study its distinctive layout. Letchworth was the first to be built in this style followed by Welwyn Garden City early in the 20th century. These were imaginative attempts to provide a pleasant environment, with tree-lined streets, in a planned new settlement mainly for residents formerly living in London.

The older part of the town has a distinct atmosphere. Ebenezer Howard was keen for each family to have its own garden and good working conditions nearby but also… no alcohol! The fact that until recently, it had just one pub, which sold only lemonade and ginger beer, says a lot about this environment. It is said that Letchworth is a lot safer to walk round at night than many towns.

This was, then, one of the original destinations for people to escape from London. An attraction is Norton Common, which is a short walk from the town centre.

Squirrels and muntjac deer are to be seen in this ideal dog-walking area.

The original garden city houses have a rural atmosphere but the town is still growing and the properties on the new estates are not as appealing. It is, though, a good place to live near, for access to its well thought of schools.

Willian

To the south of Letchworth and joined to it, is the small village of Willian, with its duck pond and some very old and interesting property. Otherwise, rural access to the south and east is restricted by the proximity of the towns of Baldock, Hitchin and Stevenage.

Hitchin

35 minutes to London Kings Cross.

Prehistoric travellers along the Icknield Way probably paused at Hitchin. Its medieval market town roots help to make its centre particularly visually attractive. Tudor and Georgian buildings surround a large market square and many narrow lanes.

It still has a large open-air market and plenty of interesting little shops as well as the usual facilities expected of a reasonable sized town. Some tree-lined roads are within walking distance of the station and at the same time, not too far from open countryside. Plenty of public footpaths lead out to Hitching Hill to the south of the town and Oughton Common, to the west.

Ickleford

Ickleford is a northern continuation of Hitchin, extending into the valley of the River Hiz. It became the Best Kept

Village in Hertfordshire in 1983 and 1985. All the old houses here are said to have the right to graze two female cattle on the common. However, take care to check this before moving in and before releasing your two cows onto it!

Considerable modern residential development has been located here but you can still take a step back in time by walking across the bridge over the river, following the Icknield Way and remembering the people who have done likewise since ancient times.

Pirton

North-west of Hitchin is Pirton, a nucleated village clustered round its church which was built within the bailey of a former castle. Countryside to the north is rather flat but hills rise to the south – up to Tingley Wood. Some interesting Elizabethan moated farmhouses are located around the edges of this village.

Hexton

Further west is Hexton, in hilly and well wooded country next to the Bedfordshire border. Its ivy covered walls, neat houses and gardens, quiet lanes and tranquil atmosphere provide a haven away from urban life. Little has been built in the village in recent times. Farming activities can be viewed from the hills to the south where the Iron Age camp called Ravensborough Castle straddles the hilltop.

Great and Little Offley

Offley – or Great and Little Offley as shown on maps – are on the top of a steep hill in an Area of Outstanding Natural Beauty. The village of Great Offley itself is not, perhaps, as picturesque as some others. Some of the old buildings have been altered and extended and there are a large number of council houses. The A505 bypasses Great Offley and provides dual carriageway access to Hitchin and Luton. Little Offley is at the end of a lane and quite remote from the hustle of modern life.

Lilley

Lilley is further west and a linear settlement on some of the highest ground in this hilly area – over 600 feet at Telegraph Hill. The shape of this village means many homes have views over verdant countryside. Lanes and footpaths such as that at Lilley Hoo, provide pleasant routes linking with the Icknield Way Path and good views into Bedfordshire.

Kings Walden

Kings Walden is really a dispersed group of hamlets rather than a village, with the Kings Walden Park estate at the centre. Even so, this scattered settlement deserves a mention, set as it is in beautiful wooded country to the southwest of Hitchin. Quiet lanes and footpaths link its several parts. The rather remote location is some distance from a station but there is a considerable choice of routes towards London – along country lanes and roads to avoid the A1 – to a choice of stations in the surrounding towns.

St. Ippollitts

St. Ippollitts is a village on the southern edge of Hitchin and sited on a hill. The village itself is quite quaint with its attractive timbered houses and a church, which provides the name for the village. New housing estates are nearby, somewhat detracting from its appeal.

To the west, in Gosmere, is Bunyan's Dell, which is a natural amphitheatre within Wain Wood where the author of Pilgrim's Progress secretly preached after the Restoration.

Great and Little Wymondley

Great and Little Wymondley are to the east of Hitchin. Great Wymondley has many thatched cottages dominated by its attractive 15th century church. Behind the church, footpaths lead to the earthworks of a former castle. Large Elizabethan homes are to be seen around the village. Queen Elizabeth II visited the beautiful village green in 1982 to present a plaque awarding the village the title of Best Kept Village. Little Wymondley is, ironically, much bigger than Great Wymondley, which has been preserved and protected from new housing developments. Little Wymondley has some interesting houses but is rather close to Stevenage New Town.

Preston

Preston is much further south, safer from the expansion of the towns and is spread along pleasantly meandering country lanes in woodland.

St. Paul's Walden and Whitwell

St. Paul's Walden and Whitwell are set in very charming wooded landscape with quiet lanes and footpaths. Early brick and half-timbered houses are of interest here, some of them dating from the 18th century.

Kimpton

Kimpton may not be described as picturesque but it does

have some pretty cottages around its village green and church plus some interesting small shops in its high street. Footpaths give access to pleasant walks in Gustard Wood. Narrow, high-banked and winding roads lead to farm-houses and hamlets with some interesting property.

Knebworth

34 minutes to London Kings Cross.

Knebworth is between Stevenage and Welwyn. The *old* vil-lage, called, unsurprisingly, Old Knebworth, is centred on Knebworth House, one of the great houses of Hertfordshire. This is of interest because its grounds are now a Country Park with picnic areas, footpaths and other facilities for enjoying this most appealing corner of the county.

The village has changed little, but *little* it is and the best chance of finding property is in the new village called Knebworth. This is very different, built round the railway station with a mixture of new housing and some older cot-tages, many of which are rather too close to the railway. Some larger houses are quite appealing and commuting is within walking distance, but the new Knebworth may not be considered idyllic.

Codicote

Codicote, to the south-west and close to Welwyn, has some attractive features in the picturesque old part of the settle-ment including chequered brick and timber-framed houses. Considerable expansion has occurred but open country is still nearby with lanes and footpaths leading down into the valley of the River Mimram.

121

Welwyn Hatfield

Welwyn Hatfield is the name given to the District including these two towns.

Welwyn Hatfield Average House Prices

Detached	Semi-detached	Terraced	Flat
429,751	226,127	179,798	130,739

Welwyn Garden City

30 minutes to London Kings Cross.

Ebeneezer Howard intended the town he designed to be self-supporting with local employment and facilities, without its residents having to travel to London. Like all the new towns, this ideal only worked up to a point and then commuting took over for many. Shops are arranged along wide distinctive routes plus the newer Howard Centre near the station. The original 'garden city' includes a spacious layout with gardens, park-like setting and cottage-style residential areas. These are popular although not necessarily the choice of those seeking proximity to the rural ideal.

Welwyn – the original old settlement – retains its identity to the north of the Garden City. Its old inns date from coaching days when they supplied changes of horse teams to keep the traffic moving – particularly The White Hart which ran its own coach service to London. Now the A1(M) has a junction here and the railway station is about a mile away. Some new developments provide a choice of homes within walking distance of open country.

Digswell

Digswell is between Old and New Welwyn. A long and large railway viaduct leads to Welwyn North station, which is, in fact, in this village. Below the viaduct is Digswell lake and an area of greenery preserved by the Digswell Lake Society – an area of 'natural beauty and tranquillity' – except for the sound of overhead trains! Nearby are a number of detached houses with unusually secluded gardens.

Tewin

Tewin has expanded nearby with substantial housing including some covetable property in the Tewin Wood area. Both villages have some wooded countryside nearby even though they are rather close to the built-up areas to the north and south.

Oaklands

Oaklands is an area of modern residential development. It has Mardley Heath to the north, a public open space of 90 acres. This was once the hideout of highwaymen. Some road names recall this: Robbery Bottom Lane, Hangmans Lane, Turpins Chase and Turpins Ride.

Ayot St. Lawrence

The Ayot villages, to the west of Welwyn, provide a much more rural environment than the edges of Welwyn Garden City. Ayot St. Lawrence is small and picturesque, reached along narrow sunken lanes surrounded by trees and hedges. The unusual church looks, from a distance, like a Greek temple. The original 12th century church was partly demolished by Sir Lionel Lyde in the 1770s because it obstructed his view from his new mansion. The ivy-covered ruined remains are left from the intervention of the Bishop, who objected to demolition and ordered Sir Lionel to build the new replacement church. Shaw's Corner is the name given to the home of the playwright, George Bernard Shaw, with its grounds open to the public in summer by the National Trust.

Ayot St. Peter and Ayot Green

Ayot St. Peter is up on a hill and Ayot Green has a splendid avenue of horse chestnut trees running through the green. This provides a way into a charming area of rural tranquillity. Attractive old cottages surround the green, conserved as most desirable homes. The Ayot Greenway is a very enjoyable walk and bridleway from Ayot to Wheathampstead with good views over surrounding countryside.

Lemsford

Lemsford is on the south-west edge of Welwyn Garden City near to the River Lea. The mill and water race are a wonderful sight here and are the 'Old Mill by the Stream' in the Nelly Dean song. An area of watercress beds, springs, osiers, reeds and pools is a nature reserve where birdwatchers can gain access to see a range of birds including kingfishers and green sandpipers in a peaceful setting.

Hatfield

33 minutes to London Kings Cross.

The New Town was built mainly in the 1950s and 60s and provides housing which is cheaper than surrounding areas but not, perhaps, the type of housing sought by the readers of this book. The traffic-free shopping centre and market provide a good range of facilities for those who live nearby. The station and nearby motorways give rapid access to London and elsewhere.

16,000 students attend the University of Hertfordshire with its largest campus in Hatfield. At one time Hatfield was a major aircraft-manufacturing centre. The university now provides much of the local employment and the former aircraft works site is being redeveloped as the new Hatfield Business Park, having been used for the location of a replica French wartime town in the film *Saving Private Ryan*.

Old Hatfield has a greater variety of house types, which may be of interest. The wooded Hatfield Park and Hatfield House are nearby to the east plus a footpath along the River Lea into pleasant open country.

Welham Green

To the south of Hatfield is Welham Green with areas of council estates and private houses. The area has open countryside nearby which, for some reason, seems to have been popular with balloonists since the Italian balloonist Vincenzo Lunardi gave the name Balloon Corner, in 1784, to the point where he landed briefly to deposit his airsick cat!

Brookmans Park

37 minutes to London Kings Cross.

This pleasant residential area has a village green surrounded with shops. There are large and desirable residences in this neighbourhood – between Hatfield and Potters Bar. Many have been built in the former grounds of mansions, near woodlands and lakes and have good views over attractive countryside.

Gobions Wood, a nature conservation area, is just to the

south and open to the public. The station is within walking distance of much of this village.

Cuffley

Cuffley (37 minutes to London Moorgate) is to the south-east of Hatfield and is another popular area for commuters. Rather more like a suburb than a village, it has many tudor-style houses and some substantial properties overlooking woodland and farms, particularly along the Ridgeway where there is access to the large Great Wood Country Park.

Northaw

Northaw is a village between Cuffley and Potters Bar. A major attraction in this area, so near to Greater London, is the good access via footpaths and country parks to the hilly and wooded countryside. The rural area is preserved as Green Belt. Muntjac deer can be seen at times even though the sound of traffic on the M25 can be heard in the distance. This was where James I and accompanying nobility hunted in the original Enfield Chase. There is the choice of two railway stations within three miles – at Potters Bar and at Cuffley, plus access to others via country lanes.

Essendon

To the east of Hatfield is Essendon, a small village with lanes and footpaths through charming valleys, farmland and woods to the hamlets of West End, Wildhill and Woodside. Many of the varied properties here are on high ground with good views. The novelist Dame Barbara Cartland lived at Camfield Place, a nearby 400 acre estate.

St Albans

24 minutes to London Kings Cross.

This is a historic town with extensions of housing estates. Easy access to and views of the countryside are limited to its fringes. On the other hand, there are some footpaths along former railway routes and the old town centre is very attractive and suitable for exploring on foot, with Verulamium Park close to the shops, providing a tranquil setting.

Plenty of Edwardian and Georgian properties are mixed with old coaching inns and cottages in this most interesting centre. Roman remains, water mill, cathedral, the traditional street market and specialist shops make this a first choice for those who prefer an attractive environment on shopping excursions from surrounding rural areas – an alternative to concrete and glass shopping malls. In particular, the Cathedral Quarter has a variety of antique shops, book, jewellery and gift shops in historic buildings with timber-framed doorways and windows decorated by medieval craftsmen.

Most of the schools are highly regarded and other facilities include over 100 restaurants, bistros, coffee shops, pubs and inns.

St Albans District Average House Prices

Detached	Semi-detached	Terraced	Flat
468,962	290,137	248,357	153,072

Colney Heath

Colney Heath, to the east of St Albans, is at the centre of a parish with the pretty hamlets of Tyttenhanger, Sleapshyde, Smallford and Wilkins Green. These make good hunting grounds for very old cottages and a variety of houses from a range of periods. Although near to large towns, the valley of the narrow River Colne has plenty of birdlife including herons and kingfishers. The remains of the heath and surrounding country is criss-crossed by footpaths that link the pubs of the parish.

London Colney

London Colney is much bigger than Colney Heath. It has a nice old village centred around the village green and river, but it has expanded greatly with much council and private housing.

Sandridge

Sandridge is strung out along the former Roman road now called the B651, extending St. Albans northwards, but retaining the characteristics of a village. Quite peaceful countryside still exists nearby.

Harpenden

32 minutes to London Kings Cross.

Harpenden has grown from a village into a haven for commuters but has done its best to keep green open spaces such as the Common with its golf courses and cricket pitch, as well as Rothamstead Park and Church Green. The schools are successful and there are many desirable properties near the golf courses and the Common. An interesting mixture of properties of different ages, sizes and prices is within walking distance of the station. Former railway tracks of closed branch lines provide access for walkers to the surrounding countryside.

There are some good village locations in the verdant rural environment surrounding Harpenden.

Wheathampsted

Wheathampsted is one of the larger villages. Its location provides a choice of routes to stations in nearby towns and a variety of country roads to avoid some of the congestion at peak times.

The appealing high street has the old quay on the River Lea near one end of it. Some very old pubs and a converted water mill add interest. A variety of buildings and houses date from Elizabethan times to the present. Country lanes and footpaths lead to Normansland Common to the south and Gustard Wood to the north of Wheathampstead.

Redbourn

Redbourn is on the other side of Harpenden. This is appealing in many ways but does suffer from the presence of the M1, uncomfortably close to the western side of the village. Redbourn Common and picturesque high street make up for this. Plenty of cottages and other varied property provide scope for finding a suitable home not far from the Colne Valley Walk running along the river and parallel to the Roman road known as Watling Street. The Nicky Way, which follows a disused railway track to Harpenden, is to the north of Wheathampstead.

Hertsmere

Hertsmere is a district in the south of Hertfordshire, including Borehamwood, Bushey, Potters Bar and Radlett. These are large towns on the edge of the Greater London conurbation but do have some pockets of countryside between them.

Hertsmere District Average House Prices

Detached	Semi-detached	Terraced	Flat
535,759	257,116	203,359	146,328

Radlett

23 minutes to London Kings Cross.

It seems Radlett likes to be called an 'urban village'. It developed mainly as a dormitory settlement for commuters and some properties on its edges overlook countryside whilst being within walking distance of the station.

Borehamwood

21 minutes to London Kings Cross.

A large town known for its Elstree film studios, there are plenty of shops serving the surrounding area in Borehamwood. The area around Haberdashers' Aske's School and Elstree village to the west of the town may have more appeal although the proximity of the M1 and other main roads could be a problem.

Shenley

Shenley, a village to the north of Borehamwood may be

more appealing. It is still separated from the London sprawl and is in a good position up on a hill. The old village lock-up, called 'the cage' is beside the attractive village pond and was used to house prisoners before they were taken for trial. The old cottages and houses here may be of particular interest. For commuting, there is a choice of stations at Borehamwood and Radlett. The M25, A1 and M1 are all within easy reach but without being uncomfortably close.

Bushey

Bushey is almost attached to the continuous built-up area of Watford to St. Albans. Part of it does still have something of a village atmosphere around its pond and church. Some quite peaceful farmland exists nearby although this is not an obvious choice for the seeker of the rural idyll.

Potters Bar

32 minutes to London Kings Cross.

This settlement mushroomed with the use of the railway for commuting. The village of South Mimms may be more enticing. It is very close to the junction of the M25 and A1(M). This could be an advantage for commuting, but not in other ways.

An attempt to improve the available open spaces is Watling Chase Community Forest. This is 72 square miles overlapping south Hertfordshire and north London around Potters Bar, St Albans, Bushey, Borehamwood and Barnet. Watling Chase consists of a mixture of public open spaces, farmland, meadows, hedgerows as well as woodland which is being substantially increased. The intention is to improve the countryside, enhance the environment and make more green spaces accessible in and around these urban areas.

Watford

24 minutes to London Euston.

This large town has the attraction of its facilities but obviously does not provide a rural environment. If being within easy reach of M25, M1 and several stations is of interest, it may be worth looking at the edges of this built-up area where there are pleasant pockets of countryside to the west and north east – in the river valleys.

Watford Average House Prices

Detached	Semi-detached	Terraced	Flat
338,069	229,222	172,098	132,824

Three Rivers

This is the name for the district at the southern end of Hertfordshire. The northern half of the district, away from the border with Greater London, has the most attractive rural environment.

Three Rivers District Average House Prices

Detached	Semi-detached	Terraced	Flat
465,988	236,454	188,072	179,011

Rickmansworth

26 minutes to London Euston.

Rickmansworth is the main town at this urban end of the county. The Grand Union Canal brought prosperity here and this, along with nearby lakes, provides some lovely waterside locations – but the main rural area lies to the north of the town.

Chorleywood

Immediately north is Chorleywood with its 200 acre common including a golf course and riding track. Some properties have views of the common and are within walking distance of the station.

Loudwater

Loudwater is just across the River Chess valley from Chorleywood. This is where the undulating, wooded area of Hertfordshire begins. The original large detached houses on quite large plots near the river are likely to be of interest. Good views can be enjoyed from here across the valley.

Sarratt

Sarratt is a village well into the cultivated farmland and woods to the north of Chorleywood and Rickmansworth. The village green is unspoilt enough to be used by film crews as a period setting. This location and neighbouring Commonwood and Belsize are some distance from a station but the rural surroundings make for a nice drive to a wide choice of stations and motorway access.

Dacorum

This is the name given to the westernmost district of Hertfordshire. It includes Hemel Hempstead, a large area to the north and west plus Berkhamsted and Tring.

Dacorum District Average House Prices

Detached	Semi-detached	Terraced	Flat
435,840	235,662	185,598	151,753

Hemel Hempstead

30 minutes to London Euston.

This New Town provides an excellent range of facilities for the surrounding rural areas, which are likely to be more appealing as places to live than the town itself. Like the other New Towns, it was built to rehouse Londoners after the Second World War.

Major routeways converge on this area after following valleys through the Chiltern Hills towards London. The M1 passes close to the eastern edge of Hemel Hempstead, and the M25 is just to the south. The railway to Euston mainline station passes the southwestern edge of the town and has two stations quite easily reached from rural locations to the west and south without driving into the town itself.

The town was originally intended to be self-contained with sufficient employment for its residents, rather than a dormitory town for commuters. Accordingly, the station is not in the centre but this can be an advantage for those living out of the town. The railway follows the line of the Grand Union Canal – which provides opportunities for boating and walking along the towpath – into a valley between beautiful areas of the Chiltern Hills. Plenty of green and hilly countryside is not far away and some properties on the western edges of the New Town may be of interest.

Potten End

In particular, Potten End is just to the west of Hemel Hempstead, and is sited next to the excellent National Trust landscape with the Ashridge Estate and Berkhamsted Common accessible via unfenced country lanes and footpaths through woodland. This village is dispersed and includes plenty of open space. The green is part of the original Berkhamstead Common. Its pretty pond sits next to the Red Lion pub, which has seating outside overlooking the water. Despite the fact that the village is 525 feet above sea level and consequently rather exposed to cold winds, market gardening thrived here at one time and some of the fruit trees and flowering shrubs remain in open spaces and gardens. Potten End is a good location to look for larger houses with substantial gardens and far-reaching views.

Bovingdon

Bovingdon village is situated to the southwest of Hemel Hempstead. The area around The Old Well is the most attractive part of this expanded village and is in a roundabout surrounded by pubs. A nearby pond is called 'Bovingdon Docks', apparently because, in the past, the locals wanted to give the impression that boats could dock here. The area has been known to flood during heavy rain but not enough to link with any major waterway!

Chipperfield

Chipperfield is between Hemel Hempstead and Watford. The village green has the traditional inn, church and small cottages nearby. Housing development has extended the village, providing a number of good sized detached houses not far from Chipperfield Common. Plenty of footpaths give access to this and wooded areas which are said to include some centuries' old sweet chestnut trees. A number of delectable old residences overlook the common and cricket field.

A few miles away is the choice of two railway stations and M25 junction 20, which is not far from the M1. Country lanes also provide access to alternative stations at Chorleywood and Rickmansworth.

Kings Langley

Kings Langley is an expanded village in the Gade Valley, where the Grand Union Canal runs beside the river, between Hemel Hempstead and Watford. This valley is rather built-up although there is the common and some open fields nearby. Some interesting old buildings are to be seen in places along the high street. The station and M25 motorway junction just to the south are convenient for commuting but uncomfortably close from other points of view. Some properties on higher ground have quite good views.

Bedmond

Bedmond village, to the southwest of Hemel Hempstead, reputedly provided a popular hiding place for the highwayman, Dick Turpin – up a chimney and onto the roof of one of the pubs. Several very old public houses still exist here. M25 and M1 motorways cut through the countryside to the south and west but some lanes and footpaths provide access to quieter country in the other directions.

Berkhamsted

35 minutes to London Euston.

Particularly attractive countryside surrounds this old market town. The Grand Union Canal environment has been greatly enhanced and the towpath provides access to plenty of picturesque rural scenes only a short distance from the town. Northchurch Common and Berkhamsted Common provide a network of unfenced lanes and footpaths through hills and woodland with views over the valley. The town is strung out along this valley, making it easy to reach the nearby open spaces.

Plenty of Edwardian and Victorian houses provide opportunities to hunt for spacious accommodation with good-sized gardens – particularly on the south side of the town where the rising ground allows good views. Some more recently built detached houses also have grounds in secluded locations. Towards the old town centre are plenty of quite attractive Victorian terraced houses. The A41 bypass and the railway pass through this valley in the Chilterns, providing convenient access to London.

Little Gaddesdon

Little Gaddesdon is a village in an area justifiably identified as an 'Area of Outstanding Natural Beauty' to the north of Berkhamsted. Most of the substantial property and cottages of this long linear settlement overlook the heathland and forest of the Ashridge Estate. Fortunately, much of the land of this Estate was purchased by local residents and given to the National Trust.

Many of the old cottages in the village were improved in

the 19th century, enlarged and redesigned with the Alford or Brownlow symbol. This, and a date outside, indicates the involvement of the aristocratic landowners in this tasteful improvement, resulting in some desirable property in excellent surroundings.

Aldbury

Aldbury village is on the other side of the Ashridge Estate from Little Gaddesdon. The old houses, thatched and timber framed cottages, church, green, and stocks and whipping post by the pond make this village so attractive it is a destination for many out to enjoy the countryside. The picturesque property here is much in demand and not easy to find for sale. It is worth enquiring, though, as it is not only a superb location but is only a short distance from Tring station and the A41 down country lanes into the valley below.

Tring

40 minutes to London Euston.

Tring has been much influenced by Lord Rothschild who provided open spaces, a meeting hall, clinic and many Victorian houses that sometimes come on the market. The Grand Union Canal Walk passes close by along a canal branch towards Wendover. Another branch of the canal goes off to Aylesbury, while the mainline of the canal carries on northwards past Tring, running near to its one-time competitor, the railway.

Be warned that Tring itself does not have a railway station. The railway runs past in the valley through the Chilterns and Tring Station is actually the name of a hamlet with a station, a mile and a half from Tring.

Wigginton

Wigginton is a village in a more rural environment up on the northern edge of the Chiltern escarpment to the south of Tring. Many of the good quality houses were built by the Rothschild family for their estate workers. More recent purchasers have varied the designs of these homes, making for an interesting mixture of styles. The village was originally the home of straw plaiters who supplied the hat industry in Luton and Dunstable with worked straw from local fields.

Access to the countryside is available on several long distance paths passing through Wigginton, including the Icknield Way, Hertfordshire Way and Ridgeway. These well-defined paths provide good views from the scarp slope of the Chiltern Hills over the surrounding countryside.

BUCKINGHAMSHIRE

Buckinghamshire is a long, roughly wedge-shaped county reaching well to the north-west, away from its short border with Greater London. The northern part of the county is beyond a one-hour train journey from London. Fortunately, the most appealing rural areas are within reach of the capital. It is in this southeast part of the county that idyllic environments can be found among the ridges and mainly dry valleys of the Chiltern Hills. The river valleys include part of the Thames valley. Substantial stands of beech forest give variety to the scenery and several long-distance footpaths help provide access to plenty of beautiful countryside.

Much of this countryside is accessible by rail, motorways and main roads and a big variety of property is available in or near many rural havens.

Buckinghamshire Average House Prices

Detached	Semi-detached	Terraced	Flat
441,293	215,659	172,964	147,449

Extracts from the 2000 OFSTED Report on Buckinghamshire Education Authority:

'At all stages of compulsory education, and for some time, the overall attainment of pupils has been well above national averages. It improved further in 1999. The schools collectively are in line to meet the targets for 2002.

The following examples illustrate the current performance of schools:

At Key Stage 2, the percentage of pupils reaching Level 4 or above in the English tests has risen steadily since 1995. In 1999 it stood at 77.6 per cent compared with 70.4 per cent nationally. Similarly, in mathematics, the percentage in 1999 was 73.6 compared with 69 nationally; at GCSE, the percentage of pupils gaining five or more grades A*-C rose from 61.3 in 1998 to 62.7 in 1999 compared with an increase nationally from 44.7 to 46.6. There is a wide variation in standards overall between schools of similar types.'

Hospitals

Some of the main hospitals include the following:

(Always check the availability of any particular medical needs carefully when visiting an area)

Wycombe Hospital covers a large area and has had new additions in recent years.

Wexham Park hospital in Slough serves much of east Berkshire. Its A&E department has recently been enlarged and the hospital has shorter waiting lists than many.

Stoke Mandeville Hospital in Aylesbury is partly being redeveloped and includes the national Spinal Injuries Unit.

South Bucks District

This district includes a large area of the Metropolitan Green Belt to the west of Greater London. In parts of this area, particularly in the southeastern corner towards the junction of the M25 and M4, it is worth being aware of

Heathrow Airport flight paths as aircraft can be low-flying in some areas. Although not as noisy as they used to be because of quieter engines and the end of Concorde flights, they can cause some disturbance.

South Bucks District Average House Prices

Detached	Semi-detached	Terraced	Flat
554,644	282,057	201,584	196,694

Iver

30 minutes to London Paddington.

Iver has plenty of 16th and 17th century houses as well as modern housing developments. The charming old part of the village is centred round the church. To the east, lakes and waterways are pleasant in parts but uncomfortably close to the M25 and industrial areas. To the west, increasingly tree-lined lanes lead to Langley Park. Iver Heath is actually a substantially built-up area but is close to Black Park Country Park with its woodlands, lake and open spaces. The nearby Pinewood Studios are where many James Bond films were made. M25, M4 and M40 junctions are only a few miles away and stations can be reached via mainly country lanes. A scattering of hamlets towards the west of Iver provide interesting places to look for country homes.

Stoke Poges

Stoke Poges has plenty of attractive open spaces around it, with commons, country parks and woodland, much of which is accessible via lanes and footpaths. It seems quite remote, being so rural, but is surprisingly close to the towns of Gerrards Cross – to the north – and the outskirts of Slough to the south. Both these towns have stations – giving a choice of line into London (33 minutes to London Paddington). Some substantial houses are to be found along tree-lined lanes and smaller homes in the newer estates.

Wexham

Wexham village is situated beside Stoke Poges on the west side of the large area of parklands including Black Park and 500 acre Langley Park. Much of this woodland area, formerly the grounds of a Royal Manor, is open to the public and popular for its beautiful rhododendrons. Wexham church is of note for being particularly old – an 11th century building with ancient timbers and door.

Farnham Common and Farnham Royal

More accessible wooded countryside is at Farnham Common, actually the name also given to a settlement beside Farnham Royal. These villages and their variety of housing are in a linear arrangement spread along the A355 which gives access to the M40 and through Slough, to the M4 and the railway there. A good choice of alternative country lanes also lead in the direction of other major routes and railways to London, in the event of delays on the motorways. The well-known National Trust beauty spot of Burnham Beeches is to the north-west of Farnham.

Cottages on cobbled lane at Thaxted, Essex

Finchingfield, Essex, ducks, village pond and green overlooked by cottages

Weatherboard cottages close to open countryside at Roydon, Essex

Canal lock on the Stort Navigation at Roydon, Essex

Lane and Cottages at Great Dunmow, Essex

Great Dunmow, Essex

Lock-keeper's house beside the coastal footpath at Heybridge Basin, Essex

Cottages overlooking the Essex coast at Heybridge Basin

Cottages on the coast at West Mersea waterfront, Essex

Seafront at West Mersea, Essex, with public pontoon and launching ramp overlooked by coastal properties

Coastal properties overlooking the coast and moorings at Mersea Island, Essex

Essex coast on Mersea Island

Houseboat on the coast of Mersea Island, Essex

Houses on Mersea Island, Essex, overlooking the coast

New flats at Maldon, Essex, overlooking the River Blackwater estuary

Sea wall footpath into salt marsh wilderness on the Essex coast

Countryside meets coast at Walton-on-the-Naze, Essex

Properties at Pleshey village, Essex, overlooking the castle moat

Sea wall, beach and seawater swimming pool beside the marina, overlooked by flats at Tollesbury, Essex

The Marina and coastal footpath at Tollesbury, Essex

Winter in the village of Little Waltham, Essex

Terling village green in Essex

Timber-framed houses near open countryside at Saffron Waldon

Saffron Walden market in Essex

Timber-framed and brick built cottages in Saffron Waldon, Essex, close to open countryside

Much Hadham, Hertfordshire, cottages backing onto open countryside

Much Hadham, Hertfordshire, variety of cottages

Timber-framed house backing onto open countryside, Much Hadham, Hertfordshire

Little Hadham village green overlooked by cottages close to Hertfordshire countryside

Country home at Little Hadham, Hertfordshire, backing onto Chiltern hillside

Substantial property backing onto open countryside at Little Hadham, Hertfordshire

Brent Pelham village, Hertfordshire, church and thatched cottages overlooking rolling countryside

Gerrards Cross

33 minutes to London Marylebone.

The town of Gerrards Cross is particularly well-sited for both commuting and rural pursuits. It has grown and gained a reputation as a typical 'stockbroker belt' location. There are plenty of substantial Edwardian and Victorian houses in good-sized gardens. The location and mainly large and luxurious property leads to this area being particularly highly priced. The local schools have a good reputation.

The M25 motorway is nearby. The M40 is even nearer and traffic noise can be a problem on the southern edge of the town. On the other hand, it could be worth tolerating this disadvantage to be within walking distance of, and possibly overlooking, peaceful wooded countryside. East Common and West Common are nearby and the 400 acre Bulstrode Park is to the west of the earthworks of an Iron Age fort.

Fulmer

Fulmer is just to the south of Gerrards Cross. This village has often won the county's Best Kept Village competition. The surroundings – around the small village green and pub – and footpaths are certainly kept in good condition. The lanes and paths provide access to the wooded Stoke Common.

Hedgerley

Another small and picturesque award-winning village, to the southwest of Gerrards Cross, is Hedgerley. Rather more modern but spacious property is on higher ground to the south of the village, which is well placed for country lane access to the M40, junction 2.

Beaconsfield

38 minutes to London Marylebone.

Much of this town appears modern but, in fact, it has two distinct sections. The old part of the town grew on the coaching routes along what is now called the A40, which is crossed here by a road from Windsor. This area has old cottages and houses dating from the 17th and 18th centuries. The part known as London End still has a village atmosphere and plenty of older buildings – including some old pubs. Junction 2 of the M40 is nearby but so, unfortunately, is noise from the motorway.

The newer section of Beaconsfield, including its main shopping centre, developed near to the railway station. The proximity of this and some successful schools are boons. Plenty of footpaths provide access to wooded countryside for those living near the northern edges of this town.

Also near the station is an unusual attraction – the oldest model village in existence, Bekonscot. This was constructed in a 10,000 square yard rock garden and shows rural England in the 1930s. Unfortunately, this village does not include homes large enough to live in!

Burnham

Burnham (31 minutes to London Paddington) is south of Beaconsfield and between Slough and Maidenhead. Although close to these large towns, it has a distinct identity as an ancient settlement on a major routeway. This is still the case with convenient access from the A4 to the M4 nearby.

The high street has many 16th and 17th century buildings and the 13th century church is nearby. North of Burnham is the 215 acre Dorneywood Estate owned by the National Trust. An even more attractive area is Burnham

Beeches just to the north of Dorneywood. This area has long been popular with poets, artists, country-lovers and... lovers. In 1773 Sheridan brought his young bride to live near here, at east Burnham. With adjoining Dropmore and Cliveden, a total of 1,300 acres are preserved from development as a natural open space and haven for wildlife.

The edges of the extensions to Burnham and the hamlets in this wonderful countryside make interesting hunting grounds for rural property.

Taplow

Taplow is a village to the west of Burnham, near to the River Thames and connected by a bridge built in 1773 over the river to Maidenhead. This provides access to the Thames Path as well as the station in Maidenhead (28 minutes to London Paddington). The cottages and church of the village are on high ground above the river valley. Taplow is known for the significant find of Saxon jewels, clothing and pottery in the grounds of Taplow Court. One of the most lovely areas of the Thames Valley is to the north of the village with wooded National Trust property. Housing includes some interesting old cottages in the village and very much larger properties beside the Thames.

Dorney, Dorney Heath and Boveney

In the much flatter landscape of the Thames flood plain, to the south of Taplow, are Dorney, Dorney Heath and Boveney. These villages are in the riverside meadows and close to boating facilities as well as walks along the path that follows the river. Risk of flooding has been reduced recently in this area, by the construction of the new Jubilee River, which takes excess water from the River Thames and helps to reduce the flood risk from Maidstone to beyond Windsor. The flow of water is regulated so the new river should not, itself, flood. If considering property in this area it is important to establish the current level of risk and ensure that insurance companies have accepted that the level of risk has been reduced.

Another advantage of the new river is the intention it should look like a natural river rather than a man-made drainage channel. It should, as its environment matures, become an attractive wildlife habitat.

The M4 passes close to Dorney Reach. This has the disadvantage of traffic noise but the advantage that junction 7 is nearby for commuting. There are two stations accessible via country lanes as well as the stations in Maidenhead and Slough.

Chiltern District

This district, in the southern half of Buckinghamshire, obviously includes an area of the Chiltern Hills.

Chiltern District Average House Prices

Detached	Semi-detached	Terraced	Flat
519,848	270,124	210,133	188,450

Chalfont St. Peter, Chalfont St. Giles and Little Chalfont

The Chalfont settlements include Chalfont St. Peter, Chalfont St. Giles and Little Chalfont, just beyond the western edge of Great London and the M25. They are situated between Gerrards Cross and Amersham.

Chalfont St Peter has won Best Kept Village accolades and has some interesting coaching inns. Its dual carriageway link with the M40 provides convenient links with London and elsewhere, and Gerrards Cross station (33 minutes to London Marylebone) is just to the south. Some access to the countryside is not far from most areas of housing.

The pretty village of Chalfont St. Giles has cottages and shops around a pond and village green. It was the 'Walmington-on-Sea' of the 'Dad's Army' film, and The Pheasant Inn was popular with Oliver Cromwell. A museum in the poet Milton's cottage and the 45 acre Chiltern Open Air Museum are likely to be aspects of particular interest. This museum collects threatened buildings of historical importance and re-erects them here. The buildings are then used to house appropriate exhibits and the fields nearby are farmed in traditional styles from centuries past. To the west of Chalfont St. Giles, lanes and footpaths lead to the Forestry Commission's Hodgemoor Woods and picnic sites up on a hill. Country lanes also provide pleasant routes to stations and motorway junctions.

Little Chalfont has housing within walking distance of its station (33 minutes to London Marylebone) and is joined to the town of Amersham.

Chenies and Latimer

Chenies and Latimer are villages to the north-east of Little Chalfont and offer an even prettier environment. Both villages are typical of the English village and are on wooded slopes above the valley of the River Chess. A number of lanes and footpaths provide good access to this valley.

Amersham

37 minutes to London Marylebone.

Amersham is to the northwest of London and is in two parts: Old Amersham and the newer Top Amersham (or Amersham-on-the-Hill). The old town attracts visitors, with its broad high street, picturesque period cottages and half-timbered buildings sited around the 17th century market hall. A market is still held here three times a week. Footpaths to the north lead to Parsonage Wood, a typical Chiltern beechwood, and to the south to Gore Hill with good views.

As well as the interesting old properties here, there are plenty of more modern homes in the newer part of Amersham up on the hill to the north of the River Misbourne valley. The end of the Metropolitan underground railway is in Amersham.

Penn

To the south-west of Amersham, Penn has plenty of footpaths through greens and woodland. It is high enough for the view from its church to include twelve counties. Many of the properties here also have fine views. The green is surrounded by well-preserved 17th century cottages.

Chesham

63 minutes via Underground to London Baker Street.

Chesham is the largest town in the district and is just north of Amersham. It has a centre nucleated on the convergence of several steep-sided chalk dry valleys and ridges. Long fingers of dwellings extend along lanes following these features to merge with linear villages including Chartridge, Bellingdon, Ashley Green and Botley. This layout gives many properties views of the green valley sides. Ridges between the valleys extend almost to the centre of Chesham providing a rural environment within easy reach of most parts of the town. Lowndes Park runs through the town centre with access to open countryside nearby. The Chess valley at Chesham does have a small river, rare amongst the dry, porous chalk landscape here.

Near the 12th century church, in Church Street, in fact, are many picturesque cottages over 300 years old. Some of the ample range of shops also occupy old timbered buildings. Larger detached properties with big secluded gardens are to be found to the south in the wooded village of Chesham Bois.

The Metropolitan underground railway line links the charming country town of Chesham with central London.

Great Missenden

Great Missenden (44 minutes to London Marylebone) and a number of nearby villages are to the west of Chesham and Amersham. Great Missenden itself is at the head of the Misbourne valley. It can be described as a small town with a long high street accommodating shops and pubs in half timbered and Georgian buildings. Church Street is particularly interesting, with its variety of older property. It leads to the 14th century church, where lanes and footpaths radiate into the countryside. As well as the railway station, within walking distance of most of this settlement, the A413 which bypasses it, provides main road access in the direction of the capital.

Plenty of recent housing surrounds the centre and can be found in the neighbouring expanded villages.

The Lee, Lee Common and South Heath

A group of villages to the northeast of Great Missenden,

151

The Lee, Lee Common and South Heath include much substantial property.

The Lee in particular has expensive large houses around its village green in a secluded and tree-lined setting. On the other side of the Liberty estate parkland is Lee Common where the properties are smaller but still in demand and therefore highly priced. South Heath provides more choice of property and many in this area have views over green and open farmland.

Wycombe District

This district of Buckinghamshire includes a large area of the Chiltern Hills. The abundance of beech wood forest distinguishes the area from that of the Aylesbury district further out from London.

Plenty of access can be found to this quite spectacular countryside via local paths and bridleways but also along the long-distance paths including the Upper and Lower Icknield Way, the North Buckinghamshire Way and the Ridgeway. In the south of the area is the River Thames with all its recreational opportunities and riverside attractions.

Wycombe District Average House Prices

Detached	Semi-detached	Terraced	Flat
451,722	210,967	179,726	140,053

High Wycombe

38 minutes to London Marylebone.

The town of High Wycombe is rather large for those seeking the rural dream. However, it has all the facilities needed by people living in nearby villages including the railway station in the town centre and access to the M40.

The town stretches along the River Wye valley. Its industries included furniture making and other activities which have resulted in a wide range of properties spreading over a big area. A range of communities have also established themselves here as a result. On the edges of the town are some attractive areas such as Loudwater, between High Wycombe and Beaconsfield. Be aware of the road noise from the M40 and congested A40 though. There are some good schools here including grammar schools that still exist in Buckinghamshire. As always, bear in mind the selection procedure for grammar schools and the effect they may have had on nearby alternatives.

To the north of High Wycombe, Hughenden Park is rated highly by High Wycombe residents. This National Trust property has grounds open to the public and leading down a slope through woodlands to a pretty valley enjoyed by the former Prime Minister, Benjamin Disraeli.

The area to the north of High Wycombe has a number of quite large villages such as Hughenden Valley, Hazlemere, Great Kingshill, Naphill, Walters Ash and Speen which provide opportunities to look for properties in more rural surroundings with plenty of glorious hilly and wooded countryside. These are well away from the busy Wye valley locations of the larger settlements and have the advantages of lanes and footpaths near to most homes. There is also the opportunity to avoid the more crowded routes towards London with a choice of country roads for at least part of the journey, perhaps heading briefly in the 'wrong' direction to a less busy railway station.

Lane End

Lane End is a popular village to the west of High Wycombe. Cottages are of interest along the high street with its pond. The M40 is too close for comfort to some properties on the northern side of this village but to the south are a scattering of interesting villages and hamlets including Moor Common, Frieth, Fingest, Rockwell End and Hambledon. These are good for secluded country homes and access to forestry commission woodland at Heath Wood and Homefield Wood.

Stokenchurch

Stokenchurch is further to the west and high up in the Chiltern Hills. Beechwoods, steep slopes and good views can be enjoyed here or nearby. The actual church at Stokenchurch dates back to the 12th century and has many striking features. Some property is too close to the M40 – or should it be the other way round? On the other hand, junction 5 is conveniently close at hand without having to drive far or through built-up areas. The motorway leads to a choice of stations at High Wycombe (38 minutes to London Marylebone) or Beaconsfield. Alternatively, more complicated but interesting routes can be taken through country lanes to Saunderton Station (45 minutes to London Marylebone) between Princes Risborough and High Wycombe.

Marlow

64 minutes to London Paddington.

South of High Wycombe is Marlow, an attractive little town on the River Thames, which here forms the boundary between Buckinghamshire and Berkshire. The high street runs down to the river and has plenty of interesting old buildings. Property beside the river itself is highly priced and rarely available but there are other properties with views over the river valley and out of reach of possible flooding.

A distinctive feature is the suspension bridge with its views of the river landscape. Near the bridge is the 'Compleat Angler' Inn which has displays featuring Izaak Walton's book of the same name. The countryside also, no doubt, helped inspire the poet Shelley, who lived in Poets' Row. A more recent resident celebrity is Sir Steve Redgrave who has won five Olympic gold medals for rowing. Not surprisingly, the town is closely associated with rowing and other boating activities. This adds interest to walks along the Thames Path.

Marlow has highly regarded schools, and others are within reach in nearby towns. These towns also provide a choice of railway routes into London although, of course, Marlow has its own station at the end of a branch line. The A404 dual carriageway and various country roads give access to the M4 to the south and M40 to the north.

To the north is Marlow Bottom, a very large area of modern housing. To the east is Little Marlow, a little village near the Thames at the end of a no-through-road and Bourne End, an area of highly desirable residences. Bourne End is a sailing centre including the Upper Thames Sailing Club. A marina and many waterside properties prove the popularity of this stretch of the River Thames. The National Trust owns and preserves much of the very scenic valley nearby.

Bourne End

Bourne End (53 minutes to London Paddington) has its own station on the rather slow branch line but there are the alternatives of driving to Beaconsfield mainline station or to one of the stations between Maidenhead and Slough to the south.

Princes Risborough

50 minutes to London Marylebone.

North of High Wycombe, Princes Risborough is 35 miles northwest of London and below the scarp slope of the Chiltern Hills. These hills provide a scenic backdrop to the east of the town.

Numerous lanes and way-marked footpaths provide excellent access to this Area of Outstanding Natural Beauty. In particular the Ridgeway Path passes the landmark of a giant white cross – Whiteleaf Cross – cut into the chalk hillside, just above Princes Risborough. The cross, visible for thirty miles, was probably cut to show the Risborough valley gap route through the Chiltern Hills to London. This route now carries commuters along the railway and the A4010 to London. As well as the station in the town, there are others at nearby Monks Risborough (57 minutes to London Marylebone) and Little Kimble (61 minutes to London Marylebone).

Princes Risborough still has the atmosphere of a sedate country market town. Annual fairs are still held in the centre of the town. Twice a year the high street and market square are the location of side-shows, rides and stalls – an enjoyable aspect for most but somewhat frustrating for motorists trying to pass through.

The property is varied and interesting. The medieval core of the town has delectable 16th to 18th century houses, some of them halftimbered and gabled. Further out are some terraced Victorian properties and more modern housing within easy reach of open countryside.

The houses become particularly large, detached and desirable towards the village of Whiteleaf, beside Whiteleaf

Cross. Being on the slope of the Chilterns, many have good views and are close to wooded countryside.

Monks Risborough

57 minutes to London Marylebone.

Once a separate village owned by a monastery, this village is now a suburb of Princes Risborough. There are some attractive old cottages huddled round the fortress-like 14th century church tower.

Housing expanded the village to merge with its neighbour in the sixties and seventies. Attractions for some are the large number of bungalows and the fact that this settlement has its own station within walking distance.

Askett, Great Kimble and Little Kimble

Further northwest from Princes Risborough are the villages of Askett, Great Kimble and Little Kimble. These provide a number of cottages and other property worth looking at, particularly if they are away from the rather busy main road and the railway line. They are close to the Lower Icknield Way and Upper Icknield Way which provide routes to wooded and hilly countryside with excellent views. The Ridgeway footpath also passes the grounds of Chequers, the retreat of Prime Ministers. Near to the villages is the station between Great and Little Kimble (61 minutes to London Marylebone). This is at the one-hour journey to London limit of this book.

Aylesbury Vale District

The substantial town of Aylesbury (59 minutes to London Marylebone) has a long history and is the county town, but little evidence of its history remains compared with many others that were originally market towns. The market square has some character but the town centre is dominated by a 12 storey tower built in the 1960s to house the County Council offices. This is known as 'Pooley's Folly' by locals, after the name of its architect. The main problem is the use of concrete for this and other buildings.

The fact that Aylesbury was once famous for the pure white Aylesbury duck indicates its rural past, but the meadows and ponds where this duck was bred were covered with council housing estates to receive overspill population from London in the 1950s. The pressure is still on to expand further and provide more housing to meet government targets – something to bear in mind if considering areas close to the town. In the Vale of Aylesbury there is not the same protection from development that exists in many conservation areas in the Chiltern Hills nearby.

Farmhouses in the surrounding countryside provide more interesting property and places to live within reach of the two railway lines and the grammar schools in Aylesbury. Check the entry requirements of these selective schools carefully before being tempted by them – and consider the alternatives.

Access to pleasant countryside is not as good as many other locations in Buckinghamshire. There is the towpath of the Aylesbury Arm of the Grand Union Canal but this leads to flat and comparatively ordinary landscape.

Aylesbury Vale District Average House Prices

Detached	Semi-detached	Terraced	Flat
331,600	181,821	155,256	111,890

Some of the villages around Aylesbury have been expanded in a similar way to the town but others are worth considering as rural retreats.

Quainton

Quainton is located to the northwest of Aylesbury where the land rises to 500 feet, giving excellent views of Buckinghamshire north of the Chiltern Hills. The long-distance footpaths known as the North Buckinghamshire Way and the Midshires Way provide easy access to both the hills and the Vale of Aylesbury. Access to railway and main roads is not as easy, but drives through the lanes may compensate for this. Quainton is, indeed, quaint, with village green, restored windmill, medieval market cross and thatched cottages – an interesting location for seekers of rural bliss.

Waddesdon

To the south of Qainton is Waddesdon, on the A41. Waddesdon Manor is owned by the National Trust. Some lovely footpaths and lanes are accessible round the wooded hill on which it stands, leading up to nearby Waddesdon Hill where way-marked footpaths meet. This village has a number of interesting old houses, an inn and a 15th century church.

Oving

Oving is to the north of Aylesbury. This village is high on a limestone hill with excellent views over the Vale of Aylesbury towards the Chiltern Hills. A square of roads round the church has a number of period cottages and farmhouses. A large network of footpaths and lanes link Oving with nearby hamlets and the villages of North

Marston, Hardwick and Whitchurch. A number of thatched and half-timbered houses are of particular interest in this area – often with good views from the hills.

Whitchurch

Whitchurch is named after the church built of white limestone. This pretty village has a good number of interesting old houses, particularly round the site of the former market where they are constructed of local stone, tile and thatch. The high street has a distinctive character with parts of its walkway raised above the road. The A413 passes through Whitchurch and descends to the Vale of Aylesbury. Another way-marked footpath called the Aylesbury Ring passes through this area and gives lower level access to the open countryside in the valley.

Dinton

A village worth considering to the southeast of Aylesbury is Dinton. The main part of this village is a short way along lanes from the A418 and therefore provides a quiet haven with lanes and footpaths radiating out over the Vale of Aylesbury. The main road provides access to a choice of stations and railway routes at Aylesbury (59 minutes to London Marylebone) and Haddenham (53 minutes to London Marylebone). The latter may be easier to access for commuting and parking.

In Dinton and some other villages in parts of this vale, are some houses built of witchert. This was the name given by the Saxons to the local earth building material often called 'cob' in other parts of the country. This subsoil is a combination of decayed Portland limestone and clay. Mixed with chopped straw and water, it produced a strong building material, built-up in layers (called berries) into walls topped with thatch or tiles. This was used

160

predominantly in the 17th and 18th centuries, although it has been used as recently as 1920.

Stone

Between Dinton and Aylesbury is Stone, strung out along the A418. The most attractive part of this village is along the lanes to the south of the main road and has some interesting timber-framed houses. Several way-marked footpaths pass through or near the village and lead to Eythorpe Park to the northwest of Stone. The hamlets of Sedrup, Bishopstone and Ford are to the south and are worth considering as rural locations.

Haddenham

53 minutes to London Marylebone.

To the southwest of Aylesbury, beyond Dinton and Stone, is the attractive large village of Haddenham with its own station. The M40 is the choice of many commuters from here and it can be reached by country lanes as well as the main roads. The southern end of the village is the old part, with the green and duck pond. This pond gave the village an amusing nickname of 'Silly Haddenham' because local folklore has it that the residents once thatched over the pond to protect the white Aylesbury ducks from the rain and splashing mud. More recently, this picturesque setting has been made famous by use in television series such as *Inspector Morse*. Another interesting aspect is the St. Tiggywinkles wildlife hospital and visitor centre of special appeal, perhaps, to families with young children.

Victorian and Georgian houses are of particular interest here and there is the choice of more modern property in the northern end of the village, within walking distance of the station.

Witchert, the white earth building material mentioned above, has been used in some walls which are capped with Spanish-looking pantiles. The Kings Head has also been built of this material.

To the north and west of Haddenham are some smaller but also charming villages including Winchendon, Cuddington, Chearsley, Long Crendon and Oakley. The first three of these are within easy reach of Haddenham station (53 minutes to London Marylebone) and in the valley of the River Thame. Footpaths follow parts of the valley and a lane runs along the top of the hills to the north, providing good views to the north and south. Long Crendon has plenty of 16th and 17th century cottages near the timber-framed early 15th century courthouse, and other interesting buildings. A choice of main roads and country lanes link with two junctions of the M40.

Brill

Brill is well to the west of Aylesbury and is of particular interest to those who like an elevated location with good views. Though rather remote compared with other villages considered earlier, its 700ft altitude provides opportunities to buy a home with a splendid panorama of surrounding countryside, either from the windows or from nearby vantage points. Plenty of attractive houses surround the village green near an Elizabethan manor house and church dating back to the 12th century. Brill windmill obviously took advantage of the exposed, windswept location on the common which surrounds the village and allows for exhilarating walking high above Oxfordshire and the Vale of Aylesbury. The drive along a choice of country lanes to the M40 junction or Haddenham station (53 minutes to London Marylebone) may add significantly to journey times but could be quite pleasant.

BERKSHIRE

The area traditionally known as Berkshire is a narrow county extending westwards from the boundary with Greater London. Scenic countryside increases westwards along the Thames Valley and into the chalk hills both north and south of the river. Windsor castle is a famous landmark.

Motorways and railways serve the area well making commuting quite rapid from many parts.

An unusual development among counties bordering Greater London is the division of the whole county into Unitary Authorities, so that Berkshire County Council has ceased to exist. These Authorities are covered in the rest of this chapter.

Reports on education authorities by OFSTED are written for each authority as the county LEA no longer exists. Therefore some extracts from these are included below. As Berkshire is not an Education Authority, schools information is included under each of the Unitary Authorities (Districts) that follow.

Hospitals

Some of the main hospitals include the following:

(Always check the availability of any particular medical needs carefully when visiting an area.)

Heatherwood Hospital in Ascot provides a range of services to the region.

Royal Berkshire and Battle Hospital in Reading is

particularly large and being extended further with expenditure of over £100 million.

Windsor and Maidenhead District

Extracts from the 2001 OFSTED Report on Windsor and Maidenhead Education Authority:

'The Royal Borough of Windsor and Maidenhead is a small and overwhelmingly prosperous authority. Located in marvellous countryside, yet close to London and Heathrow airport and therefore a prime location for business, it enjoys a booming labour market and has high property prices. Windsor Castle, Ascot racecourse and Legoland make it a magnet for tourists.

'A high proportion of the schools are church schools and over 90 per cent of all schools are judged to have good or very good climates for learning. They are popular and draw in many pupils from neighbouring authorities. Achievement is above national averages and broadly in line with similar authorities, though there are dips at Key Stage 2 and post-16. Windsor has a three-tier system of schools and there is some underachievement in middle schools.

'After becoming a unitary authority, the LEA was quick to initiate overdue action on a number of fronts. It launched a concentrated programme of promoting school autonomy and improvement through school self-evaluation, and it developed good arrangements for the support of minority ethnic children and for combating racism.

'Attainment at Key Stage 3 is well above the national average and that of similar authorities in English and science, and above in mathematics. The number of pupils gaining five or more GCSE grades A*-C is broadly in line with that of similar authorities, and well above the national average. The average GCSE points score is well above the national average, and broadly in line with similar authorities. However, the 'A' level points score for those achieving two or more 'A' levels is below the national average and below the mean of comparable authorities.'

Windsor and Maidenhead Average House Prices

Detached	Semi-detached	Terraced	Flat
518,232	262,117	231,995	196,918

Maidenhead

28 minutes to London Paddington.

Turner's painting *Rain, Steam and Speed* features Isambard Kingdom Brunel's Maidenhead railway bridge over the River Thames. This has the widest, flattest brick arches in the world and indicates the importance of transport to the location and growth of Maidenhead. Commuting over this remarkable bridge to London may not be a good enough reason to live in the area but the railway and road links certainly make the area popular with commuters. The M4 has major junctions here with the A 404, A308, A330 and (at junction 7) the A4. Villages to the north have links with the M40 and those to the south also have country routes to the A329 which joins the M3.

The original settlement grew from its location on the river transport route of the Thames and the convenient bridging point. Thus the town has an old and interesting centre plus a pedestrianised high street of character. The Thames Path provides access to the open countryside for those who may find the cheaper terraced houses of interest near the centre, but the most desirable areas are near the bridge and the river. Houses in these locations, such as Boulter's Lock, tend to be large Victorian multi-bedroom homes with good-sized gardens. As well as the Thames Path, the river itself gives good access to peaceful wooded and hilly scenery for boatowners or boat hirers.

Cookham

Cookham is a village to the north of Maidenhead, perfectly situated beside the River Thames. The hanging woods of the Cliveden Estate enhance views across the valley. Cookham itself has a village green with some interesting properties surrounding it. The artist Sir Stanley Spencer found the village appealing enough to provide plenty of suitable setttings for his paintings. Cookham Dean Common and Widbrook Common, to the south of the village are owned by the National Trust. These add to the accessibility of open fields along with numerous footpaths linking with the Thames Path.

The station at Cookham Rise (50 minutes to London Paddington) is nearby although this is on a rather slow branch line and it may be preferable to make for mainline stations at nearby Maidenhead (28 minutes to London Paddington) or the alternative route at Beaconsfield (38 minutes to London Marylebone). There is also a choice of motorways – M40 and M4 – both accessible via a choice of country lanes or A roads.

Cookham Rise and Cookham Dean

Nearby Cookham Rise and Cookham Dean provide a bigger choice of property types and plenty of access to

National Trust Commons in hilly and wooded countryside – much of it in or near the Thames Valley. Being between nearby Maidenhead and Marlow, these Cookham villages have interesting older towns for varied shopping within easy reach.

Hurley

A particularly stunning stretch of the River Thames is further west at Hurley. The river splits into several distributaries, flowing round wooded islands. Exploring these and other backwaters by boat or, partly, on foot, is a great way to spend a lazy summer's afternoon. The half-timbered cottages in the village are of interest, near one of the oldest inns in the country – the 12th century Old Bell. The ruins of an old monastery and mansion are also nearby and a more modern attraction – a marina – is on the river.

The nearby A404 dual carriageway links with the M4, M40 and a choice of railway routes into London.

To the west of Maidenhead, Pinkneys Green, Littlewick Green, Knowl Hill, Waltham St Lawrence and White Waltham villages are good hunting grounds, particularly for large detached houses in rural settings.

Holyport

South of Maidenhead, Holyport has a large village green with a pond. A mixture of cottages and large Georgian and Tudor houses are of interest here.

Bray

Nearby Bray is a smaller and more picturesque village beside the Thames. The irregular streets here have appealing timber-framed and Georgian houses. The village centre is a conservation centre always keen to do well in the

169

Britain in Bloom annual contest. Bray has the distinction of having two 3-Michelin-starred restaurants.

Large houses here, with river frontages, are popular with television personalities and are some of the most expensive properties in this already highly priced area. The flooding that has been a problem here at times should be reduced by the recent construction of the Jubilee River along the flood plain of the Thames on the other side of the river. This new channel has been designed to take floodwater from above Maidenhead to a point where it rejoins the Thames downstream of Windsor. Even so, it is wise to check with insurers that they have realised the reduced risk to property near the river.

The M4 is conveniently near to Bray and Holyport but may be a little too close to some properties.

Windsor

30 minutes to London Paddington.

Windsor is well known for its castle, royal connections and overall smart appearance. The enthusiasms of successive monarchs for the castle and its surroundings have ensured very attractive urban and rural environments close together. The town is full of character – Church Street is particularly pretty. Although smaller than many nearby towns, Windsor has a wide range of specialist shops as well as the usual chainstores.

Huge areas of semi-natural parkland are accessible in Home Park – beside the River Thames – and Windsor Great Park. These parks are natural enough in parts to be home to much wildlife, including deer, taking advantage of the extensive woodland. A way-marked footpath called 'The Long Walk' links the two parks with Windsor and The Thames Path.

An interesting combination of boating facilities and

horse racing can be found beside the river. From moorings in parts of the marina, views of the races can be enjoyed.

Much of the town centre's housing is Victorian. Towards the outskirts away from the castle, more recent semi-detached houses can be found. Part of the town is on ground above the flood plain and the Jubilee River flood relief channel provides extra protection by channelling excess water away from vulnerable areas. As always, however, there is some risk to property on any river's flood plain.

There has been some debate concerning the possible increased risk of flooding downstream of the point where this new length of river rejoins the Thames, just past Windsor – at Datchet, Old Windsor and Wraysbury – although the authorities insist this is not a significant problem. Apparently, the flooding that occurred early in the winter of 2002/3 was an exceptional 100-year event and would have affected four times as many properties if the new flood protection measures had not been put in place.

The town benefits from two stations: one on a branch line to join the mainline at Slough and the other – Riverside Station – providing an alternative route into London. The M4 Junction 6 is nearby plus alternative routes via A and B roads to the M25 and A30 or M3. Heathrow airport is conveniently accessible but can be a disadvantage in areas to the east of Windsor where aircraft noise may be an irritation.

Eton

49 minutes to London Waterloo.

Eton, just to the north of Windsor, is a small town, which grew up around Eton College, the public school founded in 1440. The presence of strangely attired schoolboys around the town makes for an eccentric atmosphere. Antique

171

shops and restaurants tend to emphasise the feeling of past being present. If this appeals, there are Victorian and more modern houses worth viewing. Much of the surrounding environment is dominated by urban rather than rural features with Slough to the north, but this is compensated for by the River Thames and views of Windsor castle to the south. Links with London are good – see Windsor above.

Datchet

51 minutes to London Waterloo.

Downstream of Windsor, along the Thames, is Datchet. This substantial, but still quite attractive, village is on the Thames flood plain, between the river and the M4. Its station is within walking distance of much of the village, and road bridges give easy access to nearby Windsor. A good choice of links with the M4 and M25 motorways via B roads and lanes give a choice of routes towards London and Heathrow Airport.

The ample access to the river is an advantage for boat owners. As well as walking along the riverside paths, boating past the many views – both natural and man-made – is one of the best ways to see the sights. It is not actually necessary to own a boat as there are opportunities to hire or to take a trip on a boat from various locations.

A wide range of property is available in Datchet ranging from smaller properties intended for first-time buyers to large 18th century houses. Plenty of Heathrow airport staff have found this a convenient place to live. The railway runs through the middle of the village where a level crossing can cause delays and the M4 is a little too close for comfort to some properties. It is wise to enquire about the present risk of flooding. Much has been done to reduce the risk further up-stream but check with insurance companies before purchase.

Old Windsor

Old Windsor, as its name suggests, is the original settlement before William the Conqueror arrived and realised the strategic value of the present site of Windsor Castle – and the advantage of a nearby forest for hunting. As successive monarchs rebuilt and extended the castle, the new location grew accordingly, leaving Old Windsor with more of a rural village atmosphere by comparison. This could be an advantage for those tired of urban living. As well as Thames-side walks and boating, there is quite easy access to the enormous Windsor Great Park – more a nature reserve than a human dominated park.

As with other settlements beside the Thames, plenty of large properties near or actually fronting the river are to be found – although whether they are for sale is another matter. They are popular with wealthy celebrities. Some cheaper properties are also to be found on housing estates.

Parts of Old Windsor are on rising ground away from the flood plain but it is worth investigating the possible flood risk if near the river and checking cover with insurance companies.

There is no station here but a good choice of stations and railway routes is available a short drive away. The M25, and M4 are accessible via a choice of routes if the more obvious A308 route to the M25 and A30 is congested.

Wraysbury

Wraysbury (46 minutes to London Waterloo) is on the opposite side of the river from Old Windsor. On a map it appears to be surrounded by water rather than countryside, with the Thames to the west and a series of lakes (landscaped former gravel pits) and reservoirs in other directions. These provide plenty of opportunities for sailing and boating generally, as well as bird watching.

Obviously it is on the flood plain of the river and previous comments about checking insurance cover apply. The railway, with two stations nearby, uses this flat land to proceed to Staines and London. Junction 23 of the M25 is also conveniently near. Also nearby, unfortunately, is Heathrow airport and the noise from aircraft which pass overhead.

A good mixture of property types can be found here, mostly built from Victorian times onwards.

Ascot

46 minutes to London Waterloo.

At the southern end of Windsor Great Park, Ascot is well known for its world-famous horse racing. Plenty of wealthy race-horse owners have large properties here; they're attracted by the golf and polo, as well as the racecourse dating from 1711 and designed to please Queen Anne. The town itself is not quite as grand as may be assumed but is nice enough. The attractions for non-horse racing enthusiasts are the proximity of the preserved open spaces and woodlands of the park, and Bracknell Forest to the south. On the edge of this forest and to the west of Ascot is a nature reserve including Englemere Pond. This area, as much of the surrounding land, was once part of the royal hunting ground associated with Windsor Castle. The pond is surrounded by a wide range of marsh habitats, enjoyed by varied wildlife and their human enthusiasts.

Although there are few traditional and undeveloped rural villages here, properties close to and overlooking the parks and forest may be of interest – expensive but also appealing.

The station provides access to London and the M3 is quite near.

174

Bracknell

64 minutes to London Waterloo.

Bracknell is Berkshire's New Town, built in the mid 20th century – not an obvious place to look for an idyllic countryside location but, of course, a shopping centre serving surrounding areas well. It is no longer the headquarters of the Meteorological Office as this has now moved to Exeter. However, many other high-tech companies have moved here in recent years.

Extracts from the 2001 OFSTED Report on Bracknell Education Authority:

'Bracknell Forest is one of six unitary authorities created by the break-up of the former Berkshire Local Education Authority (LEA) as part of the reorganisation of local government (LGR) in April 1998. It is the seventh smallest education authority, with a population of 114,000. That population is projected to grow by 20 per cent over the next decade, a growth strongly associated with the rapid economic development of the area, which is dominated by companies associated with high technology. The area is generally prosperous, but there are some pockets of social deprivation.

The performance of pupils is overall above the national average in primary schools and at Key Stage 3, and average at Key Stage 4.

The rate of improvement has been average at Key Stage 1, overall below average at Key Stages 2 and 3, and below average at Key Stage 4. Post-16 results are below the national average, and the rate of improvement is well below the national trend.

The progress made in raising standards is no better than average, and, at Key Stage 4 and above, disappointing. This is not because the LEA fails to challenge its schools suffi-ciently, nor because it has been afraid to tackle difficult issues. As a result of extensive intervention by the LEA, two out of the six secondary schools are recovering from deep-seated difficulties and are well placed for further improvement. A review of post-16 education has resulted in a well focused strategic plan.'

Many of the original villages in the area have either been swallowed up by the growth of the town or have expanded substantially, but there are locations where properties are near or overlook open country, forest or golf courses such as parts of Binfield, an overgrown village to the west of Bracknell. Locations next to the forest to the south of the New Town, known as either Bracknell Forest or Windsor Forest, may be appealing. This has over 30 parks and nature reserves as well as over 45 miles of footpaths and bridleways.

Bracknell Average House Prices

Detached	Semi-detached	Terraced	Flat
329,724	199,092	166,320	131,497

Crowthorne and Finchampstead

Crowthorne, south of Bracknell and beside the western edge of Bracknell Forest, has also expanded from its origins as a small village. Fortunately, the National Trust owns woodland at Finchampstead Ridges, which stops expan-sion of housing estates into the attractive village of Finchampstead. Some excellent views can be enjoyed from the hills in this area and it is worth looking for properties with views out over rural areas of Berkshire, Hampshire and Surrey. Much splendid countryside opens up to the west with lanes and footpaths accessing many good views. This area is midway between the M4 and the M3 and a choice of railway stations.

Wokingham

51 minutes to London Waterloo.

Sandwiched between Reading and Bracknell, Wokingham town centre has retained some of its character as an old market town. The fact that its built-up area is smaller than its neighbours means it is possible to live not far from open countryside and still benefit from the facilities of Wokingham. An advantage of the nearby large towns is the good choice of shopping centres.

The station is in the town centre, involving some effort to reach it from the outskirts. The M4 is quite near although not as easily accessible as it seems from the map, as it is necessary to drive towards Reading or Bracknell, to the A329(M), before gaining access to an M4 junction. An alternative is to turn southwest on the A329 to the M3, although this involves driving through Bracknell first.

Much of the housing beyond Wokingham town centre was built in the last half of the 20th century. Some pleasant rural country adjoins the town to the north and south, away from the sprawling urban areas along the railway line. Be aware, though, of the M4 and the busy A329(M) to the north and two railway lines to the south. These not only give some noise nuisance but tend to restrict access to parts of the open countryside.

Extracts from the 2001 OFSTED Report on Wokingham Education Authority:

'Wokingham became a unitary authority in April 1998 after the abolition of the former Berkshire County Council. The district, a blend of countryside, town and high-tech industry, is prosperous, with a thriving local economy and low unemployment. The population growth is relatively high and several new housing developments are planned. This growing population is adding to the pressure on school places. The high cost of housing within the area contributes to difficulties in recruiting and retaining staff in schools and within the LEA.

'Standards of attainment in most national tests and examinations are well above national averages. In line with its clearly stated corporate priority for education 'aiming for the highest possible standards', the LEA has set high targets for improvement for eleven-year-olds and at GCSE, and is largely on track to achieve them.

'The percentage of pupils gaining five or more GCSE grades A*-C in the 2000 examinations was well above the national average and above the averages achieved in similar authorities. The average points score of pupils at A-level was in line with the national average and the average for similar authorities.'

Wokingham Average House Prices

Detached	Semi-detached	Terraced	Flat
329,682	212,722	175,199	170,928

Winnersh

Winnersh (55 minutes to London Waterloo) is to the north-west of Wokingham. The original village has expanded to the point where it almost joins Wokingham to Reading. There are two stations here and motorway access, although the sound of motorway traffic may be irritating in many parts of Winnersh. The A329(M) has to be crossed by flyover to get to it, but Dinton Pastures Country park is accessible and full of water features. Attractive lakes provide welcome open areas here and include facilities for water sports and wildlife habitats near to the River Loddon.

Hurst

North along the valley occupied by the lakes and river, is the more attractive true village of Hurst with its village green and pond. The bowling green is reputed to have been made for Charles II.

This is where we get into the peaceful rural scene, away from the urban sprawl and motorways to the south. A mixture of properties include some good sized detached houses with country views. The landscape is rather flat here but reasonably accessible, including the River Loddon bankside path near Whistley Green and more lakes (former gravel pits) north towards Twyford.

Twyford

43 minutes to London Paddington.

This small town has a mainline station and access to A4/M4. Countryside surrounds the town and lakes prevent it from becoming a suburb of nearby Reading.

Victorian terraced houses are in the centre and near the station but still within walking distance of open country.

Larger houses can be found to the east in Ruscombe. Cheaper property is available on the housing estate but lack of adequate garden space, as on so many newer developments, may be a problem.

Hare Hatch

North of Twyford the landscape becomes more hilly, varied and rural. Hare Hatch and its hamlets Holt and Hill Green are dispersed with many properties having plenty of open space around them.

Wargrave

Wargrave (45 minutes to London Paddington) is particularly appealing. Near the confluence of the River Loddon and the River Thames, this village has plenty of riverside houses in among narrow, tree-lined lanes. Georgian and timber-framed houses add to the charm of this place, obviously appreciated by some well-known and wealthy celebrities who have chosen to live here.

The church is not as old as one might expect; suffragettes burnt it down in 1914 in protest at the vicar's refusal to remove 'obey' from the marriage vows. Such violent demonstrations are not a normal feature of this peaceful village.

There is the choice of walking to the station, which is on a branch line, or driving to Twyford for the mainline station. The nearby A4 links with the M4 via the A404(M) which conveniently bypasses nearby Maidenhead. Country lanes provide alternative routes and access to wooded countryside overlooking the Thames valley.

Arborfield, Arborfield Cross and Barkham

To the south west of Wokingham, towards the valley of the

River Loddon, the villages of Arborfield, Arborfield Cross and Barkham are worth considering. Some properties are close to and may overlook, undulating wooded country-side accessible via lanes and footpaths. California Country Park is a nearby woodland beauty spot and wildlife habitat.

Also accessible, mainly via country roads, are a choice of stations and two junctions on the M4.

Farley Hill, Swallowfield and Riseley

Particularly rural are the tiny dispersed village of Farley Hill and the more nucleated villages of Swallowfield and Riseley. These three villages are some distance from a station but are quite close to the A33, a primary route and dual carriageway that, via open country, links with the M4 where it bypasses Reading.

Reading

30 minutes to London Paddington.

Reading is a large town and an urban area likely to be avoided by those wanting to find a rural location. It does, of course, have an excellent shopping centre and university and its 'silicon valley' status, with many I.C.T. companies here, may mean employment opportunities for some.

The rural areas to the west of Reading are lovely but are on the fringe of the one-hour railway commuting time. Faster and frequent trains do run from Reading itself to London but this involves a rather congested journey from the rural areas to Reading station, and associated parking difficulties.

Extracts from the 2001 OFSTED Report on Reading Education Authority:

'Reading Borough Council serves a prosperous area with very low levels of unemployment. Nevertheless, within the compact town there is considerable diversity: substantial wealth alongside social deprivation; differing ethnic communities with an increasing number of refugees; and polarised expectations of education and employment. Schools reflect that diversity. Within the LEA are some of the most successful selective maintained schools in the country, whilst a significant proportion of others are failing to give their pupils an adequate education.

'Standards in primary schools are below those found nationally. Standards in secondary schools, boosted by the selective schools whose intake comes primarily from outside the borough, are in line with national averages, but the performance of the majority is below that found in like schools.

'At Key Stage 4, the proportion of pupils achieving five or more A*-C grades is close to the national average whereas the proportion of pupils gaining five or more A*-G and one or more A*-G grades is well below the national average.

'The average point score per pupil entered for two or more A-level/Advanced GNVQs is above the national average.'

Reading Average House Prices

Detached	Semi-detached	Terraced	Flat
308,762	193,631	152,003	135,930

The A33 to the south of Reading does provide a dual carriageway into the centre and to the station but many commuters prefer to make for Theale station.

Theale

Theale, (49 minutes to London Paddington) as well as having a more easily accessible station, is popular with businesses relocating from London – a possible advantage for escapees from London. Here we get into the district of West Berkshire, towards the limits of a one hour rail commute.

Recently there has been much enthusiasm for recreating the Victorian atmosphere of Theale, with cobbled streets and old-style lamp-posts. The River Kennet, with its accompanying restored Kennet and Avon Canal, flows past Theale to join the River Thames in Reading. Gravel pits have become attractive lakes along its valley, and canal towpaths provide a route both into the town of Reading and out into attractive landscape. Housing on the Theale (western) side of Reading has the advantage of access to this river valley and plenty of charming country lanes. The M4 junction 12 is also nearby and may be a little too close to some properties.

Aldermaston

54 minutes to London Paddington.

The village of Aldermaston, south west of Reading, has a combination of Elizabethan cottages, a wonderful 12th century church and charming properties of various ages near to the Kennet and Avon Canal. The towpath is particularly pleasant for walking, and boating on the canal is an even better way to enjoy the peaceful rural environment at a gentle pace. In particular, the canalside area of Aldermaston Wharf, a restored 18th century brick structure, with its visitor centre, makes for an interesting destination for a leisurely stroll. In all directions from this pretty village are plenty of rural areas to enjoy.

The station provides a link with Reading and its fast trains to London. The nearby A4 joins the M4 to bypass Reading.

Woolhampton and Midgham

Near to Aldermaston are Woolhampton and Midgham with its station (58 minutes to London Paddington), on the end of the one-hour commuting time to London. Unfortunately, many of the quite pleasant properties are strung out along the busy A4. Further away from the road, into Upper Woolhampton, it becomes much more peaceful, hilly and well-wooded. A network of unfenced country lanes and footpaths provide access to Buckley Common and attractive woodland.

Pangbourne

To the north-west of Reading, Pangbourne (55 minutes to London Paddington) is where Kenneth Grahame lived when he wrote for his son, *The Wind in the Willows*. The original bedtime stories were based on the nearby banks of the River Thames between Pangbourne and Marlow. This small town is at the confluence of the River Pang and the Thames. Not particularly old compared with many settlements in the area, it does have some attractive Victorian and Edwardian property.

Many waterborne visitors arrive to use the ample choice of restaurants and takeaway food providers. The water meadow and riverside paths provide access to gorgeous scenery. A rather quaint aspect is the small toll charged, since 1792, to cross the bridge to Whitchurch. On the other side is access to an area of more steeply sloping and varied country landscape on the northern side of the Thames valley.

Pangbourne station is just within the one-hour commuting range of London and within walking distance of most properties. The A340 also runs southwards along the River Pang valley to Theale, where there is another station (49 minutes to London Paddington) and access to the M4 without driving through Reading.

HAMPSHIRE

This county, to the southwest of London, has many large towns near to the border with Greater London. However, the large area of hilly and wooded countryside soon opens up to provide a big choice of interesting locations. The M3 and rapid mainline rail links help commuters to reach London.

Hampshire Average House Prices

Detached	Semi-detached	Terraced	Flat
318,182	186,991	155,103	126,073

Extract from the 2001 OFSTED Report on Hampshire Education Authority:

'Hampshire County Council serves a prosperous county, with relatively little socio-economic disadvantage. Pupils make progress in line with or above national rates and achieve good standards at all key stages.

'Hampshire is a good and improving LEA. Schools are adequately resourced and there is good corporate support for the education service.

'In 2000, standards of attainment in national tests at all key stages were above the national average. At Key Stages 1 and 2, standards were also above the average of statistical neighbours. At Key Stage 3 and 4, standards were in line with statistical neighbours.

'Over the last three years, improvement in the percentages of pupils achieving level 4 at Key Stage 2 and five grades A*-C at GCSE has been in line with statistical neighbours. Progress of pupils between Key Stages 1 and 2 and 2 and 3 is line with that nationally.

'Between Key Stages 3 and 4, pupil progress is above the national average. Recent OFSTED data show that the percentage of primary schools judged good or very good is broadly in line with the average nationally and for statistical neighbours. Corresponding data show the percentage of secondary schools judged good or very good to be above the national average and broadly in line with statistical neighbours.'

Hospitals

Some of the main hospitals include the following:

(Always check the availability of any particular medical needs carefully when visiting an area.)

North Hampshire Hospital at Basingstoke is large and includes specialist cancer treatment facilities.

Royal Hampshire County Hospital at Winchester serves central Hampshire. Around £27 million is being spent on extra facilities.

Queen Alexandra Hospital near Portsmouth covers much of the southern area of the county.

St. Mary's Hospital is in Portsmouth and also serves the southern area.

Rushmoor, including Aldershot and Farnborough

Aldershot, 49 minutes to London Waterloo; Farnborough, 43 minutes.

Rushmoor is the name given to the district of Hampshire nearest to London. It includes army married quarters and other aspects connected with the army and with the Royal Aircraft Establishment. Although this is mainly a large urban area it has some splendid woodland in the centre to the south of Farnborough Airfield. The River Blackwater valley and the Basingstoke Canal run through some lovely countryside with a number of nature reserves. A significant proportion of properties here have views over woodland, canal and river valleys. Even so, this area is not the obvious part of the county to seek the rural idyll.

Rushmoor District Average House Prices

Detached	Semi-detached	Terraced	Flat
276,354	179,822	152,860	117,271

Hart: Centred on Hartley Wintney

This district is in the northeast of Hampshire – between Basingstoke and Farnborough – and includes some pleasant rural areas. The villages of Hartley Wintney, Crondall, Greywell and Rotherwick are all past winners of the Best Kept Village in Hampshire competition.

Hart District Average House Prices

Detached	Semi-detached	Terraced	Flat
356,382	215,969	175,181	148,440

Hartley Wintney

This village boasts one of the oldest cricket greens in England. Men from Hartley played for England in the time of Napoleon. Attractive good-sized cottages overlook the cricket green and smaller Victorian cottages are to be found on the common. Some properties date from the 17th and 18th centuries.

The cobbled yards of old coaching inns are reached through archways and antique shops dominate the centre of the village. Several village ponds and greens provide an open feel to the village generally. One particularly attractive aspect is the group of old oak trees known as the Mildmay Oaks beside the village's central common. Apparently, these were planted after the Battle of Trafalgar with the intention that they should provide wood for future ships.

Winchfield station (54 minutes to London Waterloo) is just over a mile to the south of Hartley Wintney and the M3 can be reached via the A30 which passes through the village.

Hook

55 minutes to London Waterloo.

Hook, to the west of Hartley Wintney, has its own station and is near the M3 junction 5. The old part of the village has some period property but most of the housing has been built recently in estates. Despite this, it is still only a few minutes' walk from most parts of the village to verdant countryside, including Hook Common. Beyond the Common and on the other side of the M3 is the restored Basingstoke Canal.

Odiham

South of Hartley Wintney, the small town of Odiham has some very pretty old houses and cottages. Some of the half-timbered houses, with attractive brickwork, have over-hanging upper storeys.

The old stocks and whipping post, a Tudor vicarage and a restored pesthouse once used to house victims of the Great Plague in 1665, indicate the historic background of this well-preserved settlement. The remains of the keep of Odiham Castle is not far away, on the banks of the canal.

Odiham has not suffered the modern expansion experienced by its neighbour, Hook, and yet it still benefits from being within easy reach of two stations (55 minutes to London Waterloo from Hook and Winchfield stations) and the M3.

Occasionally the clatter of a helicopter can be heard from the Royal Air Force base about a mile to the south, but their presence does not seem to detract from the rural atmosphere.

A much older nearby form of transport has recently been restored: the Basingstoke Canal. A network of footpaths converge on Odiham and link with the canal towpath.

Winchfield

At the nearby small village of Winchfield there is a car park and slipway for small boats giving access to a magical and peaceful stretch of the canal. A particularly old – 12th century – church is also in Winchfield along with a quite well designed development of recent housing.

South Warnborough

Further south and rather more remote is South Warnborough. This village benefits from views over unspoilt countryside to the nearby North Downs, which rise to the highest point in the district – over 700 feet. Old brick-built and half-timbered thatched cottages are of particular interest here, not far from a 12th century church.

Long Sutton

Nearby Long Sutton also enjoys good views over surrounding valleys, particularly from the higher levels towards the Downs and from Sutton Common. The village scene includes a 13th century church, a duck pond and an attractive Tudor farmhouse. One of the oldest roads in Britain – The Harrow Way – originally ran through Long Sutton and formed one of the branches of the Pilgrims Way from the west of England to Canterbury.

Crondall

Also near the Downs and ancient Harrow Way, south of Hartley Whitney and with a choice of country roads to Farnham station, Crondall has over 80 well-preserved old houses and cottages, as well as a variety of more recent property. Queen Victoria is said to have visited here to enjoy the views from 'Queen's View' after inspecting her troops at Aldershot.

The fertile mixture of different soil types in the nearby farmland originally supported hop growing, which has now given way to more modern crops such as oil-seed rape and linseed.

A network of lanes and footpaths link with nearby hamlets and villages such as Redlands, Dora's Green, Warren Corner and Ewshot. These provide a hunting ground for rural property near to the facilities and station of Farnham. A development of large new houses at Ewshot Heights may also be of interest.

Fleet

49 minutes to London Waterloo.

On the eastern edge of Hart District, the town of Fleet has covered an area of heathland, marsh and forest beside a lake called Fleet Pond. Fortunately, the lake and its beautiful surroundings have been preserved and it is popular for angling and boating. Silver birch and pinewoods are accessible from much of Fleet. The town has its own station and the M3 is not far away.

There is a huge army presence at Fleet. A variety of housing estates built at various stages in the 20th century provide accommodation and the town is still expanding.

Crookham Village

The expansion of Fleet threatens to engulf the village of Crookham. However, it still manages to keep its title of village and has a scattering of very old timber-framed cottages. An ancient Mummers play is performed on the green each Boxing Day.

The Basingstoke Canal winds through this village and crosses the River Hart on a high embankment. Restoration of the canal has opened up access to the nearby rural environment via its towpath and, of course, by boat.

Dogmersfield

Nearby Dogmersfield village has been much influenced by the past occupants of the manor house who, in the interests of privacy, demolished most of the village and ensured the builders of the Basingstoke Canal made a wide detour. This has rather reduced the number of interesting properties here! On the other hand, the preserved parkland, Tundry Lake and peaceful rural scene provides a very relaxing environment.

Yateley

Yateley is northeast of Hartley Wintney and is a substantial built-up area. There are the remains of the original settlement in the form of a number of old buildings, some dating back as far as 1540 but much is recent development. Two stations (54 minutes to London Waterloo) and the M3 Junction 4 are nearby.

An appealing aspect of this town is its surroundings. The River Blackwater is to the north in a wide valley full of lakes. Yateley Common, a glorious expanse of well-preserved open spaces and woodland, separates the town from its neighbour, Farnborough (43 minutes to London Waterloo). The Forestry Commission's Yateley Heath Wood is to the southwest and Eversley Common is to the west. These accessible areas of open countryside make it worthwhile considering the outskirts of Yateley where there are properties with woodland views.

Eversley

Just to the west of Yateley and preferable for a truly rural location, is the village of Eversley, with its useful network of footpaths accessing hundreds of acres of nearby forest. One of several bridleways, the Welsh Drive, is the original route of the Drovers Road from Wales to the cattle markets in London. A journey to London can now be accomplished by driving through country roads to several railway stations and the M3.

Thatched cottages and larger homes, with several acres of land, are of particular interest here. Charles Kingsley, author of *The Water Babies*, and founder of the village school, was the rector of Eversley.

Mattingley

Mattingley is in a secluded location to the west of Hartley Wintney and on the other side of the large areas of forest near Eversley and Yateley. The River Whitewater flows past the village on its way to join the River Blackwater. Nearby Hazeley Heath provides good views over the river valley. The church is unusual, being built of fascinating red herringbone brickwork. It was converted from a timber-framed barn 600 years ago.

Many interesting cottages are arranged around the village green and plenty more properties can be found in idyllic rural locations scattered around the leafy lanes leading to Heckfield, Chandlers Green, Hazeley and West Green. These lanes can also be used to reach the M3 or the stations at Hook and Winchfield (55 minutes to London Waterloo) as well as the more direct A32 main road.

Rotherwick

Rotherwick is a little further west. A pleasing mixture of listed buildings and country scenery are to be found in and around this village. A well-used network of footpaths give access to rolling open countryside. A particularly popular path leads from The Coach and Horses to a ridge at Great Nightingales Copse for good views of the surrounding area. As with nearby Mattingley, M3 motorway and stations (55 minutes to London Waterloo) are a short drive along the lanes.

Basingstoke and Deane District

Basingstoke (45 minutes to London Waterloo) has expanded enormously from a market town to a large built-up area designed to take overspill population from London. Rural it is not. It does benefit, however, from a frequent train service to London and has an excellent shopping centre, which serves the surrounding villages as well as the town. The M3 draws a boundary line between housing estates and open country to the southwest, cutting off easy access to the countryside. Motorway junctions 6 and 7 are at each end of the town. On the west of the town a very much older route – a Roman road – marks the edge of most of the built-up area. This old route is now partly country lane and partly a footpath and bridleway. It provides access to open countryside from the housing estates on this side of the town.

Several hundred companies have moved to Basingstoke and may provide employment opportunities as an alternative to commuting to London. Travelling into Basingstoke from surrounding rural areas could be appealing.

Deane

Deane, although it figures in the name of the District, is actually a tiny village on the B3400 to the west of Basingstoke. Farmhouses and attractive thatched cottages are set away from the road. Overton station (59 minutes to London Waterloo) is a short drive away.

Basingstoke and Deane District Average House Prices

Detached	Semi-detached	Terraced	Flat
315,546	182,020	149,460	127,293

Oakley

Between Deane and Basingstoke is Oakley. The old village has a number of footpaths from the church into open countryside. To the east of here, are recent housing estates with two railways running through them, but no station. A drive to Basingstoke or Overton is necessary to reach a station. Access to the M3 is quite easy via a country lane to the south.

Overton

59 minutes to London Waterloo.

The village of Overton is well into pleasant countryside to the west of Basingstoke. One of the most famous trout fishing rivers, the River Test, rises just to the east, near the tiny and charming village of Ashe.

Overton is an interesting mixture of old and new. The old part of the village was actually planned as a new medieval settlement in the 13th century by Bishop Lucy of Winchester. This was a business venture – the rents from the homes constructed in a small grid of streets went to the bishopric. An even older part of the village is over the bridge near the church. A little further on, at the hamlet of Quidhampton, are watermills beside the River Test.

The older properties in and around Overton include

some thatched cottages and are likely to be of particular interest. The recent developments have extended the village substantially and provide modern alternatives quite close to rural surroundings. The station is nearby – within walking distance of the majority of properties – and country lanes provide access to the M3 at junction 7.

Whitchurch

Whitchurch (60 minutes to London Waterloo) is a small town further west and at the limit of the one-hour railway journey to London. This journey may be considered worthwhile to live close to nearby chalk downland scenery – the setting for *Watership Down* by Richard Adams.

From hills to the north and west there are good views of this area of outstanding natural beauty. In the town is the silk mill, a water mill with preserved waterwheel. Silk is still produced here by more modern methods and supplies the legal profession and drama productions such as the BBC's *Pride and Prejudice*. This is very appropriate as the author, Jane Austen, lived a few miles away at Steventon where she wrote this novel.

Whitchurch has its own station within walking distance of most homes. A quick route to the M3 is via the dual carriageways of the A34 and the A303 trunk roads, although country roads are available for a more leisurely drive.

A number of housing estates were added to Whitchurch towards the end of the 20th century, providing a choice ranging from former council houses and two bedroomed terraced houses to large mock-Tudor and mock-Georgian homes. Attractive farmhouses, several hundred years old, also come onto the market at times. A large proportion are within walking distance of the station and strolls beside the charming River Test.

Micheldever

56 minutes to London Waterloo.

Also on the limit of the one-hour journey to London is the station called Micheldever, southwest along the line from Basingstoke. Here we are just over the border into the Winchester district. The station bears the name of a village, which is actually three miles to the south. The A303 and M3 motorway are nearby and the overall accessibility of the area around the station at one time attracted attention from planners who wanted to put thousands of new homes here – possibly creating a New Town. The proposals did not get past the planning stage but there has been increased pressure from national government to find locations for 39,000 homes every year somewhere in the southeast of England and this could renew planning pressure on the area. As usual, this would provide more homes for people to buy when escaping from London, but at the same time would reduce the attraction of the rural areas affected.

Some housing has been located near the station but the older houses in the actual village of Micheldever include a random arrangement of thatched cottages round a small green and beside the headwaters of the river Dever.

Access to the wonderful former capital of England – Winchester – is easy from here, straight down the A33 which follows the route of a Roman road. Winchester may be preferable for a more interesting shopping environment than mainly modern Basingstoke. Some faster trains run from Winchester station but most of the rural area south west of Micheldever is beyond a one-hour journey from London.

North Waltham and Dummer

Some villages nearer to Basingstoke worth investigating

include North Waltham, which has easy access to the M3 at Junction 7 as does Dummer, which has a good collection of half-timbered and thatched cottages along a lane. The Wayfarers' Walk runs south from Dummer to viewpoints over the surrounding valleys – as do a network of other lanes, bridleways and footpaths.

Farleigh Wallop, Preston Candover and Brown Candover

Farleigh Wallop, Preston Candover and Brown Candover along the B3046 to the south of Basingstoke have plenty of varied rural property in charming hilly countryside with lanes connecting to the M3 and stations at Micheldever (56 minutes to London Waterloo) and Basingstoke (45 minutes to London Waterloo).

Bradley and Bentworth

Bradley, and Bentworth are rather remote but this may be their main attraction, surrounded as they are by the dry valleys of the chalk hills accessible via plenty of lanes and footpaths. The station at Basingstoke (45 minutes to London Waterloo) is within reach by the A339 or country lanes but it may be better to turn towards the lovely small market town of Alton even though its station is just beyond the one-hour rail journey limit. (71 minutes to London Waterloo)

Old Basing

This large village is just to the east of Basingstoke and likely to be preferable to living in that town. Some old properties were built partly with stones from the Tudor mansion, Basing House, which was under siege for two years by the Roundheads during the Civil War – and eventually destroyed when Cromwell himself led his men in the final assault.

Many interesting old thatched cottages are spread round the remains of this mansion, by the church and near the River Loddon. Some newer property is carefully separated from the old.

This well-preserved village is near to the M3 junction 6 and mid-way between stations at Basingstoke (45 minutes to London Waterloo) and Hook (55 minutes to London Waterloo.

Mapledurwell

Mapledurwell is a little further east but still benefiting from accessibility to London and plenty of footpaths from the lanes through the village. The thatched cottages here could provide the picturesque country retreat sought by many escaping from London.

Upton Grey

Upton Grey, a few miles south, is even more picturesque and described by some as one of the most beautiful villages in Hampshire.

The village is centred on the church of St. Mary, which has an unusual wooden exterior staircase up to the tower. Most of the houses in the village are listed as being of special historical or architectural interest. They are the types of cottages likely to be pictured on Christmas cards and calendars – particularly the 17th century thatched properties. During colder winters in the past, the duck pond froze over on winter evenings and villagers skated at night by the light of the tailor's lamp shining from his home at Pond House.

Country lanes lead to a choice of motorway junctions on the M3 and stations at Basingstoke and Hook to the north (55 minutes to London Waterloo) or Alton to the south.

Sherfield on Loddon

As its name indicates, this village, to the northeast of Basingstoke, is near the River Loddon and in very pleasant surroundings. The old mill and the village green have been restored, making attractive features. It is easy to see why it has been judged the best kept village in Hampshire. The tranquil setting and age reached by some of the residents back up the local saying, 'You live as long as you wish in Sherfield on Loddon'.

As an alternative to joining the traffic on the A33 to Basingstoke station (45 minutes to London Waterloo, Hook station (55 minutes to London Waterloo) and M3 Junction 5 can be reached by an enjoyable drive along country lanes.

Bramley

The village of Bramley (59 minutes to London Waterloo), to the north of Basingstoke, has its own station within walking distance of most of the homes here. The station is the main reason for its expansion, with a substantial amount of recent housing. It does, though, still have some of its village character with a pond, green and church providing attractive features.

Sherborne St. John

Also north of Basingstoke is Sherborne St. John. This village has done well to retain its rural character so close to the town. Duck ponds and walks beside a stream are attractions here and a number of footpaths provide access to the surroundings.

Monk Sherborne

Monk Sherborne is nearby, with its remains of a Priory and

a show of daffodils and crocuses in Spring. A peaceful setting along a lane away from the main road is combined with easy access to Basingstoke and its station, or via country lanes to an alternative railway route from the station at Bramley. Undulating wooded countryside can be enjoyed from lanes and several footpaths. The linear shape of the settlement means many properties back on to open landscape. 17th century cottages are of particular interest here.

Pamber

A little further north is Pamber. This recently expanded settlement is beside Pamber Forest, an ancient woodland where King John is said to have hunted deer. Plenty of wildlife and wild flowers populate this nature reserve which is accessible via a network of footpaths.

No railway serves Pamber but there is a choice of several stations which can be reached via a drive along country lanes.

Silchester

Silchester is near Pamber and may be preferable for seekers of the rural idyll. During Roman times it was a busy military and commercial centre but is now a peaceful village with interesting reminders of Roman times including an amphitheatre, remains of the old town and its wall. These features add interest to the peaceful, natural rural environment and are accessible by lanes and footpaths. A number of properties here are close to Pamber Forest and Silchester Common. A drive past the Roman remains, along narrow lanes, can be enjoyed on the way to Stratfield Mortimer station. Here there is the choice of a journey via Reading (30 minutes to London Paddington) or Basingstoke (45 minutes to London Waterloo).

Kingsclere

Located at the foot of the scarp slope of the North Downs, Kingsclere lies in a wooded valley between Basingstoke and Newbury, close to the limit of a one-hour train journey.

Kingsclere has had a prosperous past as a market and coaching town. This is shown in the imposing properties in the older parts of the settlement. Former mills, maltings and brewery are interesting substantial brick buildings near the river.

A main attraction of this area is the contrasting and extensive rural scenery. The chalk downs, including Watership Down, provide a chance to walk at a high level with excellent views over the other area: the wooded lower landscape to the north of Kingsclere.

Hannington

Hannington is a smaller village at a much higher altitude than Kingsclere – over 600 feet above sea level. Its hilltop location on the North Downs provides scope for seeking a property with excellent views – rather exposed perhaps, but quite possibly worth some occasional discomfort to live in a classic downland village. The parish church has an avenue of trees and the village green is surrounded by cottages and farmhouses. The ancient Portway prehistoric track runs through the village and further on passes Watership Down.

East Hampshire District including Alton and Petersfield

Contrasting rural landscapes are a particular appeal of this district. The chalk downs provide dramatic escarpments with magnificent views from open hilltops. Steep scarp slopes have woods known as hanger woodlands, with trees clinging to the rapid descent down to the vales below. At the lower levels are leafy sunken lanes and winding plains of the river valleys. Long-distance footpaths plus plenty of other bridleways and paths open up the countryside in many areas.

Just beyond the southern edge of the district, the south coast is within easy reach either rapidly via the A3(M) or, in a more leisurely fashion, along a network of lanes. This brings the south coast resorts and sheltered boating waters within easy reach.

East Hampshire Average House Prices

Detached	Semi-detached	Terraced	Flat
342,486	198,225	174,666	114,360

Alton

71 minutes to London Waterloo.

Alton has had a market in its Square for over 1,000 years and was listed in the Doomsday Book as the most valuable market in the country at that time. This gives the town centre an historic charm and attractive appearance with medieval timber-framed buildings, as well as Victorian and Georgian facades to many shops. Although there is no longer a cattle market, Tuesday is still market day with a variety of products in colourful stalls. Farmers' market days and speciality markets are also held here.

The town is named after a Saxon word meaning 'Village of the Great Spring'. The quality of the spring water encouraged the establishment of the brewing industry. The

River Wey rises here and flows off to join the River Thames.

As this is a small rural town, it is possible to live within walking distance of the station and yet be only a few minutes from the beautiful surrounding scenery. The station is just beyond the edge of the one-hour commuting journey but this may well be considered worthwhile – to live in such lovely surroundings.

Properties vary from listed 200-year-old terraced cottages to larger, more recent property and more expensive but spacious thatched houses along the many lanes that converge on Alton. The lanes also give access to plenty of footpaths into very idyllic hilly and wooded landscapes with plenty of villages to consider as even more rural locations.

Holybourne

The villages around Alton include Holybourne, which just manages to avoid being joined to Alton and retains its own identity. The village gets its name from a spring believed to rise under the 12th century church. The village is bypassed by the A31 and the station at Alton is within easy reach. Being on the edge of the built-up area, there is easy access to both the facilities of Alton and to the various lanes and footpaths leading to splendid hilly landscape.

Chawton

Chawton is just to the southwest, with its cottages of stone and thatch. Jane Austen lived in one of the cottages here with her parents. The bypass ensures a peaceful atmosphere similar to that experienced by the author. Interesting houses include the former home of the village blacksmith and one of the oldest houses in Hampshire, 'Baigens', where Elizabethan murals were discovered behind plastered walls. The Pilgrims Way, from Winchester to

Canterbury, passed nearby and there are well-signposted walks through Chawton Park Woods.

Four Marks

Four Marks, a few miles further southwest, gets its unusual name from being at the junction of the boundaries of four parishes. The distinctive feature of this quite recently developed settlement is its altitude: 700 feet up on a high ridge, providing good views for many properties strung out along the lanes. Steam trains are often to be seen working hard to ascend the slope on the restored Watercress Line.

Medstead

Nearby Medstead also has plenty of houses scattered along lanes leading down to the restored railway line. Plenty of footpaths radiate into the surrounding rural scenery, and Chawton Park Wood is close by.

Bentworth

Bentworth is along the lane northwards from Medstead. Properties here are spread along a long curve of the lane from which a number of other lanes and footpaths make it easy to get deep into rolling countryside.

Selbourne

Selbourne is a charming village to the south of Alton and is surrounded by National Trust owned rural landscape. This has helped to prevent expansion and preserve its idyllic qualities – including many properties several centuries old. It also means plenty of open space is easily accessible, such as the hilly and wooded Selborne Common. A zig-zag path up a steep slope through the forest leads to superb views over the surrounding countryside.

Attractive old properties are gathered round the village green known as the Plestor. Museums here house a surprising variety of interesting exhibits connected with rural life, natural history and by contrast, Captain Oates, the explorer. These help to emphasise the varied historical atmosphere of this special village.

The A31 and Alton station are accessible via the B3006 which runs through the village.

East Worldham and West Worldham

Another excellent viewpoint is King John's Hill near East Worldham and West Worldham. These two villages are east of Alton and provide more opportunities to find secluded rural properties with good footpath access to open countryside in most directions. The station and A31 are a short drive to Alton.

Bordon Camp and Kingsley

Further east is Bordon Camp with military installations and accommodation. The surrounding villages have been influenced by this to some extent and some of the substantially forested area is used for training exercises and rifle ranges. Kingsley retains its character with a pond and the wooded Kingsley Common. Bentley station (62 minutes to London Waterloo) is within range here via winding country lanes. The A325 provides access to an alternative at Farnham (56 minutes to London Waterloo).

Binsted

This village is to the northwest of Alton. An unusual building here indicates the good views available: The Telegraph

A classic thatched cottage at Sawbridgeworth, Hertfordshire

Village houses at Sawbridgeworth, Hertfordshire

Canal and countryside overlooked by waterside properties at Sawbridgeworth, Hertfordshire

New flats overlooking the canal and countryside at Sawbridgeworth, Hertfordshire

New flats overlooking the canal at Sawbridgeworth, Hertfordshire

Riverside walk near Sawbridgeworth, Hertfordshire

Therfield, Hertfordshire, pub and cottages overlooking the village green

Country house and The Chiltern Way footpath at Kelshall Hertfordshire

Anstey, Herfordshire, village well structure and community noticeboard

Idyllic scene in Buckland village, Surrey

Village property backing onto open views of countryside at Buckland, Surrey

Buckland village properties overlooking pond and green with Surrey countryside at rear

The River Thames at Weybridge, Surrey

View of Kent and Sussex from a home on a hill

Tile hung properties in Bletchingley, Surrey

Bletchingley in Surrey

Village post office and cottages at Bletchingley, Surrey

Cottages and country lanes at the village of Shere, Surrey

Cottages and riverside path at Shere in Surrey

Village church and cottages at Shere in Surrey

Pub at night beside Pyrford Lock on the River Wey Canal, Surrey

Stone built home at Toys Hill overlooking the Weald of Kent and Surrey.

The village of Abinger Hammer in Surrey

Cottage and country lane at the village of Abinger Hammer, Surrey

Home on a hill with a view over Kent and Sussex

Secluded bungalow — a renovation project near Sevenoaks, Kent

Converted oast house, Westerham, Kent

Hill top footpath and bridleway for horses and cyclists near Goathurst Common, Kent

View enjoyed by properties near One Tree Hill, Kent

The village of Shorne, Kent

Horse riders pass a converted oast house at Ightham, Kent riding into open countryside beyond

Houses on Ide Hill with country views in Kent

House. This was a signalling station, which forms part of a chain built by the Admiralty during the Napoleonic wars. On a clear day messages could be sent along the chain by flag signals on masts within sight of each other between Plymouth, Portsmouth and London.

The house is now a private residence. Around this village and the neighbouring hamlets including Wheatley, Wyck, Blacknest and Isington, a number of former old farmhouses are of interest and sometimes come on to the market. The distinctive local stone, called Binstead rock, has been used in some of the older properties here.

Binstead is a short drive along the lanes to Bentley Station (62 minutes to London Waterloo) and the A31. The lanes and footpaths also provide views over picturesque and wooded river valleys.

Upper Froyle and Lower Froyle

Nearer to the A31 are the villages of Upper Froyle and Lower Froyle. These were nicknamed 'The Villages of Saints' because a former lord of the manor brought many statues back from his journeys to Venice. Some of them have been adopted and placed above the doorways of village cottages and houses. In Napoleonic times prisoners of war were housed in a group of properties known as 'The Barracks'. Interesting homes are scattered along several lanes with views over the River Wey valley. A choice of footpaths exists – either along the quite flat river valley – or up the slopes to the west into the hills, for even better views.

Bentley

Bentley (62 minutes to London Waterloo) is also near the A31 and has its own station a mile to the south. This makes it a long walk from the village but means less noise from the trains. Less noise and disruption also resulted from the A31 bypassing the village. Attractive cottages and some small developments of recent housing provide a variety of interesting property along and near narrow lanes, which lead quickly into plenty of hilly scenery. To the south, the Alice Holt Forest has forest walks and picnic places. A great appreciator of the nearby countryside and its possibilities for enjoyment was Lord Baden-Powell, founder of the scouting movement, who lived near Bentley.

Petersfield

66 minutes to London Waterloo.

This ancient market town was originally planned at the end of the 11th century as a Norman new town, probably as an income-stream for local lords. The wool trade, and also the catering for as many as 30 stagecoaches a day pausing here on the way from London to Portsmouth, developed the prosperity of Petersfield.

Present day transport puts the town one hour from London by train from its station. The A3 has become a dual carriageway bypassing the town. Alternative employment may be found in the other direction, in the Portsmouth or Southampton areas, involving less commuting time by train.

The town retains its quaint old architecture. Roads leading from The Square, a former cattle market, have many 16th and 17th century buildings. The area known as The Spain, named after Spanish wool merchants who did business here, has interesting Georgian properties. A short distance from the town centre is The Heath with 80 acres of open space and leisure facilities including a boating and fishing lake. Ancient earthworks known as barrows add to the interest of this area. Large Victorian and Edwardian detached houses overlook The Heath. A variety of new developments of different styles have been added without detracting from the charm of this town. These are within easy reach of some outstanding rural scenery.

To the west of Petersfield is a hilly area sometimes called 'Little Switzerland'. Queen Elizabeth Country Park is to the south of the town along with the excellent viewpoint of Butser Hill, a peak of 889 feet in the South Downs. The Isle of Wight can be seen from this high, gorse-dotted open space on a clear day. This is a reminder that the south coast, with its sandy beaches and boating facilities, is not far away and easily reached for days out.

Buriton

Buriton is one of the oldest villages in Hampshire, with a church dating back to 1150, high on the slope above the village. This charming village is close to Queen Elizabeth Country Park and within easy walking distance of its attractions. It is beautifully situated and has a pond, interesting old cottages and a manor house. The A3 is only a mile away and Petersfield station (66 minutes to London Waterloo) a short drive to the north. Just over the border into Sussex are the Harting villages and hamlets of Elstead, Elstead Marsh and Treyford – all well worth including in househunting tours of the area near Petersfield.

Just north of Petersfield are the neighbouring villages of Steep and Sheet.

Steep

This village consists of a scattering of houses including period cottages, larger Victorian properties and some large modern houses – these last are quite unusual in having good-sized gardens. Many of these homes have good views from the slope that gives the village its name. On the other side of the common, footpaths lead into the beech woods

211

known as hangers, as they cling to hillsides. The Petersfield A3 bypass, which benefits Petersfield and some other villages, comes rather close to part of the village but the access to it is conveniently near. Petersfield station is within walking distance for the energetic.

Sheet

Sheet is a comfortable distance from the A3 bypass but within easy reach of this trunk road to London and the station at Petersfield. A very pleasant village green is surrounded by old terraced cottages, the church and pub, creating a traditional historic village atmosphere. Some quite large Georgian houses accompany two former mill buildings and a variety of more modern detached properties are to be found.

Sheet is beside the River Rother which has wooded slopes rising from its valley on the side opposite the village. The National Trust's Durford Wood and The Sussex Border long distance footpath is, of course, near the Sussex border – just on the Sussex side, to be precise. This path passes near to the village of Hill Brow – obviously located at a significant altitude.

Hill Brow

The border with Sussex passes through the village and it is included here as it is near to Petersfield. Surrounded by forested slopes, it is strung out along the B2070 and provides the opportunity to look for properties backing onto the woods. Liss station is down the hill to the northwest.

Liss

73 minutes to London Waterloo.

Liss also provides interesting properties – some of them with several acres and views of the forested slopes nearby. The station is within walking distance of most of the village but somewhat beyond the one-hour range of London. Although not as quaint as some other villages in the area, there is a good housing stock here including Victorian houses ranging from terraced cottages to large detached properties in the Liss Forest area. Slightly cheaper are the modern detached houses.

Liphook

67 minutes to London Waterloo.

Liphook is between Petersfield and the Sussex town of Haslemere. This is not a picture book village but it does have its own station and the A3 bypassing it. The Square, with its impressive 17th century Anchor Hotel is a conservation area but most of the housing is of recent terraced and semi-detached style with some detached homes in parts. The outskirts, including Bramshott, Conford and a number of hamlets, could yield a covetable property beside wooded countryside. Just north and east of Liphook, National Trust land at Bramshott Chase, Ludshott Common and Waggoner Wells provides peaceful open spaces and wooded walks. Further, easily accessible, hilly forested areas are nearby to the south and east into Sussex.

To the west of Petersfield, there are few large villages on the steep slopes but there are some very small villages such as Oakshott and High Cross and some hamlets and farmsteads for those seeking solitude.

East Meon

There is the village of East Meon, a particularly attractive nucleated settlement slotted in below one of the peaks of the downs: Park Hill. Lanes and footpaths radiate from the village giving a choice of gently sloping walks or a steep climb up Park Hill or Small Down – which is actually rather large to those not used to steep slopes... The South Downs Way long distance footpath passes to the west with spectacular views over the downs.

Interesting old properties date back as far as the 1300s including 16th century thatched cottages and good sized Tudor and Victorian homes. Some modern large houses are well to the south with good views towards the English Channel. Winding narrow lanes, or the A272 to the north of East Meon, provide access to the A3 and Petersfield station.

East End and West Meon

Further to the west is East End – the author claims no connection with this name! This hamlet and neighbouring West Meon village are rather remote from railway stations but the busy A32 passes, quite disruptively, through West Meon. Thatched houses and semi-detached, recently built, houses are within easy reach of rural slopes either side of the River Meon which flows through the village. As the stations within reach are at the edge of the one-hour journey to London, these villages are at the south-western limit of this book.

SURREY

Surrey is possibly the most highly regarded county in the area around Greater London. As with other counties, there are large towns near to Greater London but the countryside is very peaceful and well-wooded, particularly close to London, bringing some of the best rural environments within easy commuting distance of the capital. This, of course, has long been realised and helps to explain the high house prices in most parts of this county.

Surrey Average House Prices

Detached	Semi-detached	Terraced	Flat
475,718	238,477	205,765	169,415

Extracts from the 2003 OFSTED Report on Surrey Education Authority:

'Surrey is a large county with very low unemployment and a mainly affluent population. Only one ward is amongst the most disadvantaged 20 per cent nationally, although there are pockets of comparative disadvantage that affect particular schools in other wards.

'Surrey has many strengths, no weaknesses and aims for excellence in all that it does. The current extent of good or very good work demonstrates that it is well on the way to achieving its ambition. It has built effectively on the strengths identified at the time of the last inspection, and has addressed the recommendations rigorously.

'Standards in schools are high, although the LEA recognises that there is room for further improvement at Key Stage 4, post-16 and in the attainment of vulnerable groups, such as looked after children. At Key Stage 1 and Key Stage 2, results are well above national averages and above those of similar authorities. At Key Stage 3 they are above the national average, but in line with those of similar authorities. Attendance figures are above the national average and the rate of exclusions is broadly in line with national figures.'

Hospitals

Some of the main hospitals include the following:

(Always check the availability of any particular medical needs carefully when visiting an area.)

Ashford Hospital works with nearby St. Peters Hospital in Chertsey providing around 600 beds.

Frimley Park Hospital in Frimley is a large hospital serving the west of the county.

Kingston Hospital in Kingston-upon-Thames is known in particular for its day surgery provision.

Epsom General Hospital provides a wide range of facilities.

Royal Surrey County Hospital, Guildford serves west Surrey and is being thoroughly modernised.

East Surrey (Redhill) and Crawley Hospitals work together and make a large combined facility.

Spelthorne Borough including Staines, Ashford and Sunbury

On the map this most northern district of Surrey looks mainly built-up, or blue. The blue areas indicate numerous reservoirs, lakes and the River Thames, which marks the district's southern and western boundaries. This is not an obviously idyllic rural area but it does have pockets of very attractive semi-rural environment – particularly near to the water features. The northern edge borders on Heathrow airport with some obvious disadvantages.

To the south and west, though, are the riverside villages which are featured below. Sailing and other types of boating take place on the various waters in the area. The Thames also provides bankside footpaths and leisurely access for boat owners to some gorgeous countryside. The Thames locks have colourful, landscaped surroundings, as do the parks and other open spaces beside the river. Marinas and boatyards provide the necessary facilities and moorings.

Unfortunately the otherwise magical presence of the river brings the disadvantage of the risk of flooding. Exceptionally wet winter periods have caused 'once in a hundred years' flooding events recently. It is wise to investigate any possible risk to a property of interest and to check insurance cover is available at a reasonable rate.

Spelthorne Borough Average House Prices

Detached	Semi-detached	Terraced	Flat
358,317	222,517	194,551	154,686

Staines

Staines (37 minutes to London Waterloo) is not a village but has been an important bridging point on the Thames since Roman times and has a large shopping centre. Away from the main built-up area, varied, interesting and expensive properties overlook the River Thames. Staines has a station, of course, but it may be found preferable to make for one of the other stations in less busy areas. The 37 minutes journey to central London is a distinct advantage of this location. In addition the A30, M3 and M25 junctions are nearby. The M25 here is even busier than elsewhere but the addition of more lanes should help.

Laleham

Laleham and Shepperton retain village features near to the river. Laleham has many attractive 18th and 19th century properties; there is also a 17th century pub and a church dating back to the 12th century. Semi-rural open spaces are accessible in several directions including Laleham Park, the former grounds of Laleham Abbey, near the River Thames.

Staines station is a short drive away but congestion may make it preferable to make for an alternative such as Shepperton station (51 minutes to London Waterloo).

There is a choice of main road routes towards London including dual carriageways linked with the M25 and M3.

Shepperton

Shepperton (51 minutes to London Waterloo) has much pleasant riverside scenery with islands in the river and many meanders. Not surprisingly, plenty of properties have been erected on the riverbanks. Some of them originally were holiday or weekend homes but have been improved to become full time residences. In some cases the only access is by boat – for building materials as well as residents. This can add to the charm of the environment but, as mentioned previously, take care to investigate the level of flood risk. Many accept this as an occasional hazard – most of the time floods may do no more than waterlog the garden – but insurance companies may not be happy with this attitude.

The features that do their best to control the river water – weirs and locks – are an attraction in themselves, being kept in good condition and surrounded with careful, colourful landscaping. A great variety of vessels, including picturesque varnished slipper launches and other traditional craft powered by steam or silent electric motors, mingle with the narrow boats, sailing dinghies and cruisers on a sunny day. The river is not as crowded as some waterways – such as the popular parts of the Norfolk Broads – and plenty of space remains for new residents to use boats on the river. The full-time lock keepers will advise on licences, regulations and facilities. Boat hire is available at a number of points on the river.

The towpath is a very popular walk. Access to both banks varies as one side is private on some stretches, but it is possible to cross the river in places by passenger ferry – in gaps between road bridges – such as the one that crosses to the Weybridge side near Shepperton lock.

Shepperton's Church Square leads down to the river and has 400-year-old pubs and restaurants as well as a variety of old and characterful properties.

Littleton

Away from the river is Littleton with the Shepperton studios nearby where *Shakespeare in Love* was made, among many other films. One of the reasons for this location being chosen was the nearness of rural, semi-rural and city locations for filming scenes away from the studios. Littleton has one of the oldest and most attractive churches in south-east England: the parish church of St. Mary Magdalene, built in 1135. Unfortunately, other old buildings were replaced with more recent housing developments before conservation became established.

Sunbury

48 minutes to London Waterloo.

Many of the period buildings in Sunbury were replaced some time ago with office blocks and shopping precincts. There are some very smart Georgian properties and the riverside has its appeal, but commercial activities are prominent here and the edge of the Greater London conurbation is obvious.

Runnymede Borough including Egham, Chertsey and Addlestone

This area has towns and villages on one side near to the west bank of the River Thames, and substantial open spaces on the other side of the area. Here Windsor Great Park, Virginia Water and various forested areas combine to make an extremely leafy environment, mainly just over 40 minutes train journey from central London.

Runnymede Borough Average House Prices

Detached	Semi-detached	Terraced	Flat
496,812	229,234	199,175	170,319

Egham

43 minutes to London Waterloo.

Runnymede meadows, where the Magna Carta was signed in 1215, is an attraction here as a place for relaxation in lovely surroundings beside the Thames.

Egham has its own station and easy access to M25, M3 and M4 motorways plus the A30. Some pretty cottages and other covetable property can be found near the bridge over the river although the area is rather built-up. Many Victorian houses are to be found in the town and a number of estates of recently built property are quite close to the rural areas to the west.

Englefield Green

Englefield Green provides rather more interesting property just to the west of Egham. The large and attractive green was preserved by the influence of the wealthy property owners surrounding it. There are certainly some large and attractive properties here, overlooking the green and within walking distance of very much larger area of greenery – Windsor Great Park. Fortunately there are also smaller, more affordable, properties here too, such as appealing terraced cottages. The Coopers Hill area is high above the Thames valley and provides excellent views over Runnymede.

Virginia Water

46 minutes to London Waterloo.

The actual lake was created by the Duke of Cumberland in the 18th century as an ornamental feature, which can now be enjoyed by all. The area links with Windsor Great Park, and a longer walk can be taken up to the hill overlooking the Royal Palace of Windsor.

Property in the exclusive Wentworth Estate is large, luxurious and expensive, home of many media and sports celebrities. Homes that do not overlook the golf course are a little cheaper, and in the semi-rural atmosphere of Virginia Water village are some more realistically priced properties. The village has a station. The M25 and M3 join near here but access to them is not quite as straightforward as may be assumed on glancing at a map.

Thorpe

This village is beside the M25 but is still a popular place to live. Attractions include a good number of large houses with good-sized gardens and the nearby Thames with a large area of boating facilities at Penton Hook Marina. There is a choice of stations nearby. The motorways and nearby lakes tend to restrict access to open countryside but the proximity of Thorpe Park Theme Park may be an attraction to some families.

Chertsey

54 minutes to London Waterloo.

This town is between Egham and Weybridge, beside the Thames and between the M25 and M3. It also has a station. This accessibility has caused Chertsey to expand from its old origins, evident in the buildings in the town centre and around the bridge. Victorian houses and cheaper flats may be of interest. Much of the centre has been improved with substantial refurbishment recently. This includes some new homes above shops and offices within walking distance of the station, but not in rural surroundings.

Open countryside is nearby and there are delightful open spaces preserved within and near the town, such as

Gogmore Farm and Chertsey Meads which include 170 acres of riverside land. To the north is St. Ann's Hill, a 250 foot high viewpoint. This overlooks Thorpe Park Theme Park from a distance that some may prefer. The wooded area around the hill makes for a pleasant environment overlooked by some properties, including large detached houses on the outskirts of Chertsey. Unfortunately this area is also rather close to the motorways, and traffic noise may spoil the rural scene for some.

Lyne and Silverlands

The villages of Lyne and Silverlands are to the west of Chertsey and offer rural surroundings within quite easy reach of the motorways and Chertsey station (54 minutes to London Waterloo) – although a drive along country lanes to the station at Virginia Water (46 minutes to London Waterloo) may be preferable. Property here is in demand because of its location rather than its age and historical interest. Some is Victorian but most is modern.

Addlestone

51 minutes to London Waterloo.

The town of Addlestone developed with the coming of the railway. Some Victorian homes were built in Station Road and nearby streets but there followed a massive expansion during the 20th century. Local industry flourished, originally making wooden propellers for early aircraft. The nearby M25 attracted new industrial estates, which can be the source of out-of-London employment opportunities with high-tech companies.

There is a quite appealing area beside the Wey Navigation where the large mill at Cox's Lock has been converted into numerous flats. Many of them overlook the large mill pool, canal, lock and meadows where livestock graze between the canal and River Wey. Unfortunately, the housing estates of New Haw and Woodham come between this area and the glorious scenery further west and south along the canal towpaths. However, in the other direction, the Wey valley is picturesque where the river and canal proceed to join the River Thames at Weybridge.

Elmbridge Borough including Weybridge, Walton-on-Thames, Esher and Cobham

The northern part of this district is heavily built-up although there are some pockets of semi-rural open space and charming walks beside the River Thames, which forms its northern boundary.

Further south there are wider gaps between towns with unspoilt river valleys and some commons. South of Cobham is truly rural.

Elmbridge Borough Average House Prices

Detached	Semi-detached	Terraced	Flat
653,000	293,442	255,913	207,674

Weybridge

28 minutes to London Waterloo.

This area has been popular with royalty for many centuries. They established estates which now give their names to residential areas such as Oatlands Park. This once was the location of a palace where Henry VIII married his fifth wife, Catherine Howard. The palace was demolished and the stone was used in the construction of the waterway known as the Wey Navigation, one of the oldest canals in the country. This canal and its river reach the River Thames at Weybridge. Although much of the area is built-up with highly priced property, the areas around the rivers Wey and Thames are peaceful and semi-rural in parts. Wooded islands in the river are overlooked by a number of properties ranging from small timber-built bungalows to mansions with gardens sweeping down to the river.

Boating activities include canoeing, rowing and sailing as well as the motor cruisers and canal boats. Membership of the town's sailing and boating club, with admittedly basic facilities, costs surprisingly little and is in a terrific setting on the Thames, beside other clubs catering for tennis and ladies' rowing.

To the south of Weybridge, is St. George's Hill. This large area of luxurious properties arranged around a golf course is the location chosen by a number of successful entertainers and other well-known personalities. It is an expensive, exclusive and secure haven for the wealthy.

Islands in the River Thames

Islands have an appeal of their own. Living on one is the ultimate detached and peaceful existence. Along this part of the Thames some islands ('aits' or 'eyots' as Thames islands are often called) are nature reserves and uninhabited though fun to visit by boat for a picnic, paddling or swimming if permitted.

Others are suitable for dwellings. Some examples include Trowlock Island which is downstream from

Kingston-upon-Thames, Thames Ditton Island, upstream of this town, near Hampton Court, Taggs Island near the lock at East Molesey, Sunbury Court Island, Hamhaugh Island at Weybridge and Pharoah's Island in Shepperton. At one time, Lord Nelson owned Pharoah's Island, which was given to him in recognition of his success at the Battle of The Nile. He took his beloved Emma there for fishing trips.

The original structures on Thames islands were mainly holiday homes built early in the 20th century. Since then most of them have been enlarged and improved or rebuilt to become suitable as permanent homes.

It may still be possible to find one of the original small timber holiday homes on an island for between £200,000 and £270,000. Redeveloped/rebuilt properties can be twice that or much more.

Waterside properties are generally priced 30% to 50% higher than similar nearby properties away from the river. Often a mooring for a boat on the Thames is included with a waterside property. This brings much extra enjoyment and has considerable value in itself.

On the islands, price also depends on the desirability of the exact location. The advantages of a magical, secluded riverside setting have to be compared with some disadvantages. Road bridges connect some islands but others are only accessible by boat. Some are pedestrianised, which means cars have to be parked before walking over a bridge to the island. Car parking may be a problem. Goods having to be loaded onto a boat before being taken to homes on an island with no vehicle access, could complicate deliveries to properties. However, those determined to enjoy the novelty and delights of being surrounded by water are often prepared to overcome such inconveniences.

The most obvious risk is flooding. Many redeveloped properties have been raised and protected from flooding as much as it is possible to do so. The weirs and other structures help to control flooding and many new flood protection measures have been installed in recent years.

Local council planning offices should be able to advise on the flood risk to actual properties. The '100 year event' is often referred to, indicating the level of risk. Insurance companies are another matter. The situation concerning the availability of cover and the cost needs to be checked carefully before considering purchase.

Bearing in mind the special delights of living on an island, including boating and fishing from the garden, many residents are prepared to accept the inconvenience of the river occasionally coming too close for comfort and flooding gardens and roads.

Byfleet

Nearby Byfleet (33 minutes to London Waterloo) comes down to earth with the usual range of properties in a commuter area near London. Both Weybridge (28 minutes to London Waterloo) and Byfleet have stations, and rail travel is likely to be preferable to taking to the rather congested roads – many of which have speed ramps where short cuts seem possible.

Open countryside adjoins the southern edge of Byfleet and continues beyond the M25.

Walton-on-Thames, Molesley, Esher and surrounding settlements form an extension of the London suburbs. Nice as parts of these towns are, they are not rural.

The common between Esher and Cobham opens up some attractive wooded spaces but the continuous countryside starts south of Cobham.

Cobham

35 minutes to London Waterloo.

On a meander of the River Mole, the old part of this town has an interesting watermill, a number of older properties and a 12th century church. The working watermill is on an attractive stretch of the River Mole, where a salmon ladder helped salmon leap up-river in stages round the weir.

The valley of the River Mole to the south of Cobham opens up rather flat but quite picturesque countryside, including the 160 acres of Painshill Park. This incorporates the restored Hamilton Landscapes - works of art with trees, and water features adding variety to the valley side.

A considerable variety of property is to be found to the north of the old village area, some of it well spaced out with large gardens and backing onto woodland. Various commons and heaths are accessible by lanes and footpaths.

The A3 is to the west and the station at Stoke D'Abernon is nearby.

Stoke D'Aberon

Stoke D'Aberon (35 minutes to London Waterloo) is joined to the western side of Cobham. Most of the property here is within walking distance of both the station and open countryside. A number of footpaths and a lane connect with the well-wooded Great Bookham Common to the south of the River Mole valley.

Oxshott

31 minutes to London Waterloo.

Oxshott station is the next on the line towards London from Stoke D'Abernon. Plenty of good sized properties are spread over a large area within walking distance of the station and close to the beautiful Oxshott Heath. The heath provides wooded surroundings for horse riding, walking and bird watching. More open space extends over the river valley to the south – although interrupted by the M25 – and into woodland to the east. Among a number of historical properties is the Highwayman's Cottage, built in the 16th century and probably occupied by Dick Turpin or other highwaymen at some stage in the past. He would find the highway here now very busy and difficult to cross at times.

Woking Borough

31 minutes to London Waterloo.

Woking is a large town with all the facilities one would expect to find in a settlement of this size. The urban nature of much of the town may not appeal but it is surrounded by plenty of verdant countryside. Its station is placed in the centre of the town with frequent fast train journeys into London, and the M25, A3 and M3 are not far away. The town is a busy commercial centre with traffic to match. However, locations on the outskirts may provide access to main routes via country roads, avoiding the built-up areas.

Much of the north side of the town has council house estates. The other areas, particularly towards the southern edges, provide a good range of different property types, most of it built fairly recently. Plenty of lanes and footpaths provide access to the meadows and farmland of the River Wey valley, where the National Trust owns the canal running parallel with the river. The Basingstoke Canal passes right through Woking and parts of the towpath offer scenic walks, eventually reaching well-wooded countryside to the west. Boating is, therefore, an attraction in itself and for 'gongoozlers', as lockside spectators are affectionately called by boaters. Occasionally a horse-drawn barge takes paying passengers along the Wey canal.

Woking District Average House Prices

Detached	Semi-detached	Terraced	Flat
461,923	227,279	180,736	145,428

Pyrford

A marina, pub and lock combined with the towpath, are attractions near the small village of Pyrford, east of Woking. This village is located in meadows and has some attractive brick built cottages near the church.

Old Woking

Old Woking, is nearby. As its name implies, it has a number of characterful older properties. As the Basingstoke canal and the railway bypassed Old Woking to the north, more recent development took place there, leaving Old Woking with a quiet village atmosphere. The old church is near the River Wey and footpaths run from the nearby river bridge across the fields to the canal.

Mayford, Sutton Green and Worplesden

Mayford, Sutton Green and Worplesden, west of Old Woking benefit from having Worplesden station (33 minutes to London Waterloo) nearby as an alternative to reaching Woking station along busy roads. The landscape is also quite rural here and not far from the station are good-sized properties spread through wooded countryside with large gardens or plots of several acres. Some open spaces such as Whitmoor Common and Jordan Hill are nearby.

Brookwood

Brookwood is west of Woking. Its station was originally built to serve the huge cemetery with one-way journeys from London for the victims of typhoid in the 19th century. It is now a commuter station with a less morbid service to the capital (37 minutes to London Waterloo). Many properties are arranged along the Basingstoke Canal and there is a reasonable choice of recently built homes within walking distance of the station.

There is some access to open countryside, including the canal towpath, but access overall is limited to a certain extent by the rifle ranges and so on, associated with Pirbright Camp to the west.

Surrey Heath including Camberley, Frimley and Lightwater

As the name implies the area has heath as well as woodlands and farmland. Substantial areas are available for recreation and rambling but large sections are also occupied by army training activities.

Surrey Heath Average House Prices

Detached	Semi-detached	Terraced	Flat
383,216	214,400	183,893	174,235

Camberley

71 minutes to London Waterloo. From Farnborough, 43 minutes to London Waterloo.

This town was established from the mid 19th century when the Royal Military Academy was located at nearby Sandhurst. Some of the larger properties built to house officers remain but many were replaced by higher density housing in this military town. The station is placed to serve the town's original function and the more recently constructed M3 runs along the south-eastern edge, close to many properties. This is not an obvious location for those seeking the rural idyll.

Frimley and Frimley Green

Frimley, just the other side of the M3 from Camberley, is an area of recent housing estates. Frimley Green has more of a country atmosphere with some period property in parts. The park next to the canal provides a route along the towpath away from the built-up area. To the east there is woodland and some rights of way but much of the area is used for training activities associated with Deepcut Barracks and Pirbright Camp.

Frimley station (75 minutes to London Waterloo) is within walking distance of the mainly recently built property although a faster journey may be achieved by driving to Farnborough station (43 minutes to London Waterloo) for the rail route via Woking.

Bagshot

Bagshot (65 minutes to London Waterloo) is northeast of Camberley and a much smaller settlement than its neighbour. Care has been taken to preserve Victorian-style lampposts and other period features, giving a distinctive character to the old centre of the original village. The expansion of housing around it may lack period charm but does provide well-situated homes for commuters.

A number of large houses back onto open land or forest.

Lanes and footpaths lead into pleasant countryside in several directions although the railway and motorway obstruct access to some extent.

Bagshot station is a short walk from many homes here but some residents prefer to drive to stations at Brookwood (37 minutes to London) or Woking (31 minutes to London Waterloo) for the faster journey on that line into London. Alternatively, Junction 3 of the M3 is close to Bagshot.

Lightwater

Bagshot Heath and the nearby Donkey Town indicate rural characteristics near the M3 and railway at neighbouring Bagshot.

The Lightwater Country Park has 143 acres of natural beauty including heathland and woodland accessible by way-marked footpaths from the adjoining areas of housing. The hill, called High Curley, provides good views from its footpaths. This makes up for some of the heath to the south being labelled 'Danger Area' on maps because of army activities.

Although much of the housing in Lightwater is rather ordinary, it is within easy reach of the open rural areas mentioned above.

Windlesham

Windlesham, to the east of Bagshot, is much more attractive than other nearby settlements. Some timber-framed and thatched houses can be seen here, in addition to many Victorian homes of various sizes. Some have large grounds and ample facilities as well as views over rural areas. Modern development that is evident in neighbouring settlements has not had a large impact here.

Chobham Common is to the northeast and plenty of lanes and footpaths run into pleasant wooded countryside.

Bagshot station and the M3 are nearby.

West End and Bisley

West End and Bisley are between Bagshot and the western end of Woking, with Brookwood station (37 minutes to London Waterloo) within a short drive along the A322. In the other direction is convenient access to the M3.

These large villages are surrounded by heaths, farmland and Bisley Common. A mixture of properties of various sizes – mostly comparatively recently built – are spread along a roughly north-south line with open countryside to be seen from many properties.

Chobham

Chobham is between Bagshot and Woking – close enough to use the facilities of Woking but separated by substantial rural landscape. Here we have traditional old property one might hope to find in a rural village, dating back to the 16th century. The high street has antique shops and a rather nice hump-backed bridge over the small stream called The Bourne. The church dates back to the 11th century.

Chobham Common is a large and peaceful open area to the north with a network of footpaths and bridleways. Chobham Place Woods are on the edge of the common and accessible from a variety of good sized properties over-looking parts of the common.

A choice of country roads and lanes provide access to the M3 and the station in Woking (31 minutes to London Waterloo).

Guildford Borough

41 minutes to London Waterloo.

As well as the attractions of this large and historic town, the surrounding countryside, including the Surrey Hills Areas of Outstanding Natural Beauty, has a number of idyllic locations.

The town has plenty of interest in among cobbled streets and old buildings, particularly along and near the high street. It has a well known modern cathedral and university. The cathedral and the castle are located high enough to enjoy panoramic views. The site of Guildford is partly on a hill beside a gap between the Hog's Back ridge and the Downs to the east. The River Wey breaks through the ridge here making a routeway used since ancient times. This puts some of its housing on quite steep slopes with good views in many directions. The town has expanded with housing estates so some parts may not suit the seeker of a rural environment. However, there are areas of interest on the outskirts, overlooking hilly and wooded countryside and not too far from the station.

The River Wey Navigation is one of the earliest canals of its type to be built – 350 years ago. The canal was replaced by the railway for faster goods transport but is now owned by the National Trust and fully used for leisure purposes. Eventually 'London's Lost Route to the Sea' will be restored right down to the south coast via the former Wey and Arun route. Parts of the canal path provide diverting walks within the town and out into the country, along with the opportunity to take boat trips or hire craft. A traditional horsedrawn boat carries passengers at times in the summer.

Comparatively rapid and frequent trains connect the town to London, and the A3 dual carriageway is nearby.

Guildford District Average House Prices

Detached	Semi-detached	Terraced	Flat
490,654	233,104	214,895	160,904

Send and Ripley

The neighbouring villages of Send and Ripley are to the northwest of Guildford and on the other side of the River Wey from Old Woking. The station in Woking (31 minutes to London Waterloo) is nearer than Guildford's station and the A3 is nearby. Pubs were built near the canal firstly for the 200 men who built the waterway and later to serve the barge families who worked and lived on their horse drawn vessels. This canalside location also attracted some industry and housing, such as can be found in the village of Send. The land is flat and open but quite pleasant beside the canal and river, with a number of footpaths and lanes leading to the canal and nearby villages, such as Ripley.

Ripley

This village has interesting brick and half-timbered houses along the curving high street and near to the village green. Formerly a staging post on the route to London, Ripley is now bypassed by the A3 dual carriageway. A quite serene drive along country roads gives access to a choice of stations at Byfleet, (33 minutes to London Waterloo) Horsley (42 minutes to London Waterloo) and Effingham (38 minutes to London Waterloo). Wisley Common is just to the northeast, with open spaces and woodland. For the keen gardener, is the added bonus of living near to the Royal

Horticultural Society's gardens at Wisley.

East Horsley, West Horsley and Effingham

A horseshoe-shaped arrangement of housing areas to the east of Guildford includes the two Horsley settlements. The layout means many of the quite recently built properties are overlooking or within reach of wooded countryside accessible via numerous lanes and paths. The dip slope of the North Downs escarpment rises to its crest to the south providing views over the dry valleys of the chalk hills. This is a particularly scenic area to look for that country cottage. A choice of two stations, Horsley (42 minutes to London Waterloo) and Effingham, (38 minutes to London Waterloo) are within walking distance or a short drive of many homes.

East and West Clandon

East Clandon, a little nearer to Guildford, is a lovely village with a number of timber - framed and brick cottages along its winding main road and near the church which has a large and particularly old bell tower. Other buildings that contribute to the charm of this small village include a 17th century farmhouse and an old forge. The most attractive scenery here is to the south – the North Downs rise to their crest before dropping away steeply where the lane down Combe Bottom plunges through forest to reach open views over the Weald. The nearest station is a short drive to West Clandon (47 minutes to London Waterloo), which has grown thanks to its station, with some developments of recent housing and properties strung out along the A25 partly between New Park and Clandon Park. Again, the best scenery is just to the south where the A25 diagonally descends Albury Downs – part of the North Downs – with excellent views from it and the nearby footpaths. Shere and

Gomshall villages are below this steep slope, in a sheltered south-facing situation.

Shere

Shere is one of the most picturesque villages in Surrey. A good selection of old and interesting properties are to be found near the 12th century church. To the north, the North Downs Way passes National Trust land, which includes part of the ancient Pilgrims Way and Crackway on the steep scarp slope of the Downs with excellent views. These are views that would have been enjoyed by pilgrims on their way from Winchester to Canterbury in Chaucer's time – except for the modern additions such as the railway and A25, which nowadays provide travellers with many times faster journeys including connections to London via Guildford (41 minutes to London Waterloo) to the west.

An alternative to the London-bound A25 and A3, is via country lanes, and includes an interesting drive over the Downs from Shere northwards to join the A3 near Ripley.

Southwest of Shere are partly unfenced lanes leading to small villages and hamlets such as Albury, Albury Heath, Brook, and Farley Green, with many secluded properties in idyllic countryside.

Gomshall

Gomshall village is a former centre of cottage industry, once busy with tanning and leather-making and with a number of Victorian properties. A pretty 15th century pack-horse bridge crosses the River Tillingbourne here. The old water mill originates from the 11th century and now houses antique and craft shops as well as a restaurant. Locations away from the rather busy A25 may be preferable. Gomshall has a station (63 minutes to London Victoria), although a quicker train journey to London may be achieved by driving to an alternative on the mainline such as Guildford station (41 minutes to London Waterloo). Like its neighbour, Shere, it has plenty of steep footpaths with good views on the nearby North Downs and a large number of interesting, although rather highly priced, properties spread out into the rolling hills to the south.

Chilworth

Chilworth (55 minutes to London Waterloo) is just over the hills to the southeast of Guildford. Gunpowder was made here and an accidental explosion demolished the old church in the mid 19th century. It was rebuilt in Norman style. Fortunately there is no longer any risk of properties being destroyed by accidents at the munitions factory. It is no longer producing explosives but the building is open to the public.

It may be that other old properties were destroyed along with the church for most of the present houses and bungalows are less than 100 years old and are unremarkable.

The location of Chilworth is quite appealing. Fine viewpoints rise to the north and are easily accessible via several footpaths. To the south is Blackheath, partly owned by the National Trust. A network of footpaths run from the village into this wooded hilly area, which has an atmosphere of remote charm. There are also some characterful Victorian properties scattered in this area.

The station is within walking distance of many properties in Chilworth, and the A248 runs through the village. It is possible to reach the London-bound A3 via either the A25 or country lanes to the east, thus avoiding a drive through Guildford. The route via lanes includes an interesting drive over the Downs from nearby Shere northwards to join the A3 near Ripley.

Shalford

51 minutes to London Waterloo.

South of Guildford and only just separated from it by the Tillingbourne, where it flows into the River Wey, this village has a number of interesting cottages and period dwellings. A village green and a particularly attractive, old watermill add to the appeal of this village. The mill was restored by a rather eccentric and secretive group known as Ferguson's Gang. They later donated it to the National Trust.

Near Shalford is the junction of a canal running from the Wey Navigation down to the River Arun and the south coast. Enthusiasts are doing an excellent job of renovating this waterway. As well as the present and future boating opportunities along the Wey, the old canal route's towpath is open, in parts, for access to a large part of the 36 miles southwards to the sea.

Modern transport routes also merge near here to go north through the gap in the North Downs formed by the River Wey. This river was powerful and determined to flow northwards, as it eroded down through ancient rock layers, regardless of their resistance, to superimpose itself on the landscape as it appears today. The A281 and the railway from Shalford station now follow this river-made route into Guildford and onwards to the A3 and London.

Compton

To the southwest of Guildford is Compton. This is another old village with a particularly fine church partly dating from Saxon times and containing a hermit's cell and 800-year-old murals. On the subject of paintings, Compton is well known as the home of the 19th century artist G.F. Watts, whose memorial gallery contains 200 of his artistic works.

The Hog's Back ridge forms a steep slope just to the north of Compton. The A31 dual carriageway follows part of the ancient Crackway route along the top of the ridge and joins the A3 to bypass Guildford. Many old and interesting properties have, nearby, the footpaths known as The Pilgrims' Way and the North Downs Way. These run parallel along the foot of the ridge passing close to the village and providing good access to some wonderful rural scenes.

Puttenham

Also close to the ancient footpaths and A31 is Puttenham, just to the west of Compton. Access from both villages is available via country roads and lanes to a choice of nearby stations for the journey to London. This area is equidistant from several large towns, where it may be possible to gain employment as an alternative to the commute to London. This would involve a short drive through rural tranquility rather than the journey into the city.

As well as the viewpoints from the Hog's Back, a delightful network of lanes and footpaths also extend southwards into wooded, rolling countryside.

Puttenham and neighbouring hamlets have a particularly appealing mixture of weathered old properties. Part of their attraction is the combination of local building materials. Chalk changes to sandstone here and this shows, mingled with red brick and tiles, in the walls of the 15th to 18th century houses.

Seale, Sandy Cross and The Sands

Nearer to Farnham than Guildford, the villages of Seale, Sandy Cross and The Sands actually have the remains of sand pits and quarries where the sandstone was excavated for the construction of their cottages. Crooksbury Common is to the south, providing wooded hilly views, and plenty of good properties overlooking this rural area. Stations at Farnham (56 minutes to London Waterloo) and Aldershot (49 minutes to London Waterloo) are a short drive to the west, as well as easy access to the A31, leading to the A3.

Ash, Ash Green, Flexford, Wood Street and Wanborough

North of the Hog's Back ridge, where the land flattens out to the west of Guildford, are Ash, Ash Green, Flexford and Wood Street. These villages are near to Wanborough station (56 minutes to London Waterloo), which is actually beside Flexford, with many properties there within walking distance of the station, and a short distance from the rising ground to the south – providing excellent views from the Hog's Back. In the actual hamlet of Wanborough is the smallest church in Surrey, dwarfed by a large monastic tithe barn. Access to the countryside is rather restricted in places to the north where 'Danger area' signs appear on maps and on notices when the army is exercising near Aldershot.

Pirbright

This village, to the northwest of Guildford, has managed to retain much of its rural character despite expansion as a result of the coming of the railway. The unusually large village green has many old listed properties overlooking it. Colourful gardens and an 18th century pub beside a stream enhance the special atmosphere of this village. A number of lanes and footpaths run from the village into partly wooded commons and towards the Basingstoke canal, with its towpath. Parts of the area further to the northwest are dominated by the army's Pirbright camp and its rifle ranges, but in other directions are hamlets set in woodland – particularly towards Worplesden.

Worplesden

33 minutes to London Waterloo.

This village is spread out among heaths and woodland in a peaceful environment. Unfenced lanes go through the woods to Worplesden station, two miles from the actual village centre.

Property here includes charming 18th century brick built houses, surrounding the village green, up on a hill. A number of interesting houses with large gardens or several acres of paddocks are tucked away in the woods. Whitmoor Common is to one side and Guildford is nearby.

Epsom and Ewell

Epsom grew as a spa town on the reputation of its spring water and the Epsom salts obtained from it. Its high street has attractive old buildings and a Victorian clock tower, making it a delightful shopping centre. But this is a built-up borough and not a rural environment. It has attractive parks such as Nonsuch Park at Ewell and Horton Country Park to the west. Epsom Common and Ashtead Common also provide plenty of open spaces plus woodland. It may be that properties overlooking these are of interest, particularly as they could also be within walking distance of one of the stations serving the area. Countryside begins to open up more to the south, where Epsom Downs – famous for the horse race course – Woodcote park and Walton Downs provide hilly rural scenes in the dry valleys of the North Downs. These areas are also near stations, (36 minutes to London Waterloo) and not far from the A217 dual carriageway towards London. There are, in fact, several large towns around this pocket of countryside, where employment opportunities may be available to reduce travelling to work. An example of a local employer is Pfizer

Pharmaceuticals. Their offices were recently relocated to Walton-on-the-Hill, where their state of the art offices have been built in serene wooded surroundings to the south of this area.

Epsom and Ewell Borough Average House Prices

Detached	Semi-detached	Terraced	Flat
380,436	254,921	195,385	175,426

Mole Valley District including Leatherhead and Dorking

This is a large district centred on Dorking and with Leatherhead, Ashtead, Fetcham and Bookham forming the main built-up area at the northern end near to the beginning of the Greater London conurbation. Much of the rest of the district provides a good hunting ground for rural retreats.

A substantial section of the North Downs are between Leatherhead and Dorking with plenty of wonderful hilly landscape and views over the River Mole Valley. This valley cuts through the chalk Downs providing a routeway from Dorking northwards for road and railway links to London. Southwest of Dorking, hills rise again, this time of sandstone, providing even more striking and well-wooded rural scenes and viewpoints.

A feature of the sandstone is the sunken roads in some parts. Horse-drawn carts and carriages eroded the quite soft sandstone away in places, with their hooves and narrow wheels. The sand was then washed away by rain-water lowering the level of the track below the surrounding land. The former tracks are now surfaced, preventing further excavation, but these lanes often seem to burrow through the landscape under a canopy of trees and then suddenly reach a breathtaking viewpoint overlooking the Weald to the south.

The National Trust owns and preserves many of the nicest areas, providing car parks and well-maintained footpaths.

Mole Valley District Average House Prices

Detached	Semi-detached	Terraced	Flat
472,169	255,650	215,184	160,906

Leatherhead

45 minutes to London Victoria.

This town is a substantial size, with the housing estates of Ashtead extending the built-up area to the northeast plus Fetcham and Bookham to the southwest. Some forest and open farmland to the north separates the urban area from the more continuous conurbation fringing Greater London. The most interesting countryside is to the south – into the North Downs and the River Mole valley. This valley has the railway with a station at Leatherhead and several main roads converging on the town, linking up with the nearby M25 and A3.

Leatherhead itself has retained some of its character, with buildings dating back to the 16th century in the narrow streets of the old part of the town. The main area for rural property-hunting is to the south – along the valley of the river Mole – as there are few villages on the higher parts of the North Downs. Although this may be frustrating it means the countryside remains rural rather than built-up! You cannot have your cake and eat it.

Mickleham

This village, in the Mole valley, is particularly picturesque. Its atmosphere has been protected by the traffic being diverted round it along the A24, which also provides a dual carriageway northwards. This road can be used to reach Leatherhead station (45 minutes to London Victoria). Alternatively, lanes provide a short drive – or long walk – to the station at the more rural Westhumble (51 minutes to London Victoria). Steep footpaths and lanes give access to the high points of the Downs – to Box Hill in particular.

Box Hill

The village of Box Hill is some distance from the actual viewpoint and country park, but it does give plenty of access to delightful wooded landscape and excellent views across the Weald to the South Downs in Sussex.

Westhumble

Westhumble (51 minutes to London Victoria) has grown up alongside its railway station in the Mole Valley. Mainly recent properties here are located near to the North Downs Way long distance footpath. This runs parallel with the ancient Crackway and Pilgrims' Way from Winchester to Canterbury. The National Trust provides plenty of open spaces along these paths which follow the scarp slope of the Downs.

Dorking

53 minutes to London Victoria.

This town has ancient origins resulting from its location on converging routeways. It is still the centre of road and rail routes, making it convenient for commuting. Some old buildings remain, helping to create the attractive built-up environment in the centre including properties in parts of the high street, West Street and North Street. Much of the town is Victorian, including some interesting houses arranged round a green beside South Street.

An advantage of Dorking is the proximity of very pretty unspoilt surrounding countryside within a short distance of most properties.

North, Mid and South Holmwood, and Holmwood Corner

Much has already been mentioned about the Downs to the north of Dorking. To the south is Holmwood Common with a network of footpaths across National Trust land and four small villages called North, Mid and South Holmwood plus Holmwood Corner, which is close to Holmwood station (60 minutes to London Victoria). The A24 dual carriageway links these villages together and also provides access to London for Beare Green and Capel. Recently built housing is to be found in the villages mentioned above – housing which is very close to excellent countryside. This includes, to the west, the highest point in southeast England: Leith Hill. A tower was built on the top of this hill to reach 1000 feet above sea level and to give superb views over the trees in all directions.

Ockley, Forest Green and Walliswood

South of Leith Hill are many small settlements and farm-houses in undulating and scenic countryside. These include Ockley, Forest Green and Walliswood.

Much of the sandstone hilly area around Leith Hill has been protected from development, so properties are rare and isolated but often in idyllic locations where it is, some-times, possible to find one for sale.

Westcott

More villages and housing developments occur on the lower ground to the west and east of Dorking – such as Westcott, which is, not surprisingly, to the west.

Westcott is one of the villages on the junction between chalk and sandstone, where both types of stone have been used, giving a varied appearance to the older buildings.

Abinger

Further west are the Abinger villages and common. These are particularly old settlements with evidence of Stone Age dwellings from 5,000 BC. The 12th century church was partly destroyed by a flying bomb during the second World War and was later damaged again by lightning – hence the evidence of careful rebuilding.

Abinger Hammer

Abinger Hammer is the strange name for one small village. This area was the centre for the manufacture of cannonballs from locally excavated iron ore, using charcoal made from the extensive forest. It is almost unbelievable that this peaceful and picturesque part of southeast England was once an industrial centre of iron-working ringing to the sound of hammers driven by waterpower – hence the name of the village. A reminder rings out every hour from an unusual clock, which features a man hitting a bell with a hammer. Properties are few but interesting in such a location as this – between the Downs to the north and the sandstone hills to the south, rising up to the magnificent viewpoint of Leith Hill.

The A25 and Gomshall station (63 minutes to London Victoria) are also nearby.

Brockham

This village, to the east of Dorking, is arranged round a triangular green on which cricket is played – on some occasions in the past by W.G. Grace. A well-attended Guy Fawkes bonfire celebration also takes place on the green.

The collection of desirable, mainly 18th century, properties around the green is most appealing and includes cottages as well as large properties with plenty of space around them. Views up towards the heights of Box Hill can be enjoyed from many points here and a track crosses the railway line to give access to them.

Dorking station (53 minutes to London Victoria) and the A25 are a short drive from Brockham.

Betchworth

Betchworth (56 minutes to London Victoria) is a little further to the east, between Dorking and Reigate. Many properties here are spread along lanes with open countryside behind them. They include appealing 17th and 18th century cottages. Other characterful buildings range from the 15th century Old Mill Cottage to manor houses. The valley of the River Mole is quite flat here but the land rises steeply into the Downs to the north, with footpaths and lanes providing access.

251

Betchworth has its own station within walking distance of most homes here. The journey is one hour to London so we have reached the limit of coverage in this district.

Reigate and Banstead District

Rather like the Mole Valley district, this sub-region of Surrey stretches from the built-up area around Banstead and close to Greater London, south through the open area of the North Downs and on to lower lying verdant country-side to the south of Redhill and Reigate. Unfortunately the M25 and M23 motorways have carved up parts of the chalk hills of the Downs – particularly where the two motorways meet and then cut into the steep scarp slope. However, plenty of attractive, accessible countryside remains. The scarp slope to the north of Reigate includes Reigate Hill, which is part of a long stretch of National Trust land with good views.

The River Mole meanders between Reigate and Horley in an area of scattered hamlets and farmhouses as well as more recent developments near to the London to Brighton railway, which also serves Gatwick Airport south of Horley.

An advantage of the motorways, main roads and railways converging on this area is the accessibility of London and other areas where employment may be found.

Reigate and Banstead District Average House Prices

Detached	Semi-detached	Terraced	Flat
453,670	221,004	201,589	148,328

Banstead

38 minutes to London Victoria.

Banstead is at the beginning of the countryside on leaving the London conurbation. It has some of the atmosphere of a country town and its expansion has been constrained by Green Belt regulations. Banstead has its own station, and the first mile of the journey to London is through the open space of Banstead Down before reaching the urban sprawl beyond. Many properties are within walking distance of both the station and rolling downs with open fields and woodland.

Tadworth, Kingswood and Walton on the Hill

More housing extends to the south with Tadworth, Kingswood and Walton on the Hill surrounding Banstead Heath and its many footpaths. A variety of properties here overlook wooded countryside, and many of these are within walking distance of railway stations. The A217 runs through the area and links with the M25, as well as providing a dual carriageway towards London.

Reigate

50 minutes to London Victoria.

Reigate is in the middle of this district with plenty of beautiful countryside around it. The town has a good mixture of Georgian and Victorian buildings in its high street. Some older buildings add interest elsewhere in the town centre.

Housing estates have extended the town in many directions and some parts of these have easy access to very pleasant rural areas such as the hills reached by the Greensand Way footpath to the west of the town, Reigate Hill to the north and Earlswood Common to the south.

There are some large detached properties in the vicinity of Reigate Hill, with good-sized plots.

Reigate has main roads providing a choice of routes northwards and its own station, but neighbouring Redhill has a station on the mainline with a more rapid journey (34 minutes) to London Victoria.

Redhill

Redhill (34 minutes to London Victoria) adjoins Reigate to the east. This town grew after the arrival of the railway in 1841. Much of the residential development dates from the 1930s onwards and includes plenty of good-sized semi-detached and detached houses, in some cases at lower prices than in Reigate. Access to countryside is available in some directions from property within walking distance of the station.

Earlswood and Salfords

To the south of Reigate, housing developments are strung out along the railway through Earlswood, with its station (44 minutes to London Victoria) and common, and Salfords, again with its own station (47 minutes to London Victoria).

Horley

Horley (32 minutes to London Victoria) is a town in flatter countryside south of Reigate and just north of Gatwick Airport. Much recent housing is here and the town continues to expand. It benefits from the motorway and railway links that serve the airport but care should be taken to investigate the level of aircraft noise that may affect any property under consideration. Expansion of the airport is also a future possibility.

To the west of the railway from Horley to Redhill, a number of hamlets offer substantial properties with large gardens or paddocks. These include Reigate Heath, Leigh, Mynthurst, Irons Bottom, Wrays and Norwood Hill. Plenty of scope exists here for finding a secluded property in idyllic countryside not far from a railway line and main roads to London.

Tandridge District including Warlingham, Caterham, Oxted and Lingfield

This is a large district including plenty of splendid open countryside. Caterham and Warlingham in the north of the district are quite large built-up areas, but fingers of rural land extend into them and then the North Downs really open up further south and to the east. The rest of the district is mainly rural. Parts of the area provide opportunities to get away from it all and may even be considered a little remote. However, the M23 runs up the western edge of the district, Redhill mainline station is to the west and other railway access to London serves the eastern side via Lingfield and Limpsfield.

Tandridge District Average House Prices

Detached	Semi-detached	Terraced	Flat
453,670	221,004	201,589	148,328

Caterham

43 minutes to London Victoria.

This is a town that grew as a result of the railway branch line arriving from Purley and terminating here as well as the establishment of army barracks. The barracks have since closed and the area is being developed as an 'urban village'. Much of the town is quite modern.

Harestone Valley has large houses in a woodland setting. Another interesting area is to the south where Gravelly Hill rises from the built-up area to open hilly countryside on the crest of the North Downs. The North Downs Way gives access to plenty of good rural views to the east and west.

Warlingham

Warlingham (35 minutes to London Victoria) is to the east of Caterham and has a more rural atmosphere to some of its streets, although some old cottages have been submerged in new housing. Stations are within walking distance of many properties, which also have some wooded hillsides nearby.

Woldingham and Woldingham Garden Village

South of Warlingham, Woldingham Garden Village and Woldingham itself provide many properties spread among woodland and rolling downland hills. Lanes lead to the high viewpoints of the North Downs just to the south, where plenty of National Trust land and ancient footpaths provide access.

Oxted

38 minutes to London Victoria.

The original old village of Oxted has an attractive collection of pubs, restaurants, shops and some 400-year-old houses. A substantial part of the property, though, is of more recent Victorian and 20th century construction. This provides an interesting mixture within easy reach of the station and close to most appealing hilly countryside. Many of the properties are well spaced out with large gardens – a feature lacking in many towns and expanded villages in the crowded parts of southeast England.

Oxted station's arrival sparked the comparatively recent growth of the new areas of Oxted. Plenty of interesting specialist shops line the central roads of this 'new Oxted'.

Hurst Green

Hurst Green (37 minutes to London Victoria) extends Oxted southwards and is centred on a pretty green. Again, the station caused expansion and the village joined with Oxted. Variety is available in the quite recent properties and it is worth exploring the various options in different parts of Hurst Green. Like Oxted itself, most properties are within walking distance of both the station and pleasant open countryside. In particular, to the south is Merle Common, Staffhurst Wood and to the east, the National Trust's Limpsfield Common. These are particularly picturesque areas of countryside with wild life and wild flowers in abundance at certain times of the year.

Limpsfield, Pains Hill and Limpsfield Chart

Limpsfield village is just to the east of Oxted (38 minutes to London Victoria). Some of the buildings in the village date back to medieval times. Old stone-built cottages are in evidence in the high street and the ancient rural village atmosphere is appealing. As usual, Oxted station has attracted areas of more recent housing within walking distance.

Around the old village itself, plenty of footpaths and lanes run out on to Limpsfield Common where large properties overlook wooded countryside: particularly at the nearby hamlet of Pains Hill which has good views from its hill. Limpsfield Chart village is also interesting for rural properties with good views nearby, and access to the common land and wooded hills here called High Chart. Groups of stone built cottages are of interest. Many of the houses near the common are large with good-sized gardens, tennis courts, and so on, and with prices to match.

Tandridge

This settlement's name is used for the District of Tandridge, despite it being quite a small village. Pleasantly situated to the southwest of Oxted, Tandridge is mainly built on the south-facing slope of a hill. A good mixture of old and newer properties provide opportunities to live in a typical village environment. A footpath called the Greensand Way runs through the village. This is named after the correct term used for the sandstone rock that forms many of the hills of this area. It provides access to Tilburstownhill Common to the west and Limpsfield Common, on the other side of Oxted, to the east. Country lanes are used to reach the A22 and the stations at Hurst Green or Oxted (38 minutes to London Victoria).

Crowhurst Lane End, Crowhurst, Haxted and Arden Green

Some hamlets and farmsteads are scattered over the delectable undulating rural scene around the headwaters of the River Eden, to the south of Tandridge, such as Crowhurst Lane End, Crowhurst, Haxted and Arden Green. These are worth exploring for more secluded rural property within quite easy reach of stations (38 minutes to London Victoria) and main roads. The churchyard in Crowhurst has a yew tree thought to be 4,000 years old – one of the oldest in the country.

Godstone

Godstone is between Oxted and Redhill to the west, near to the M25 junction with the A22. This helps to provide access to road and rail routes into London but has the disadvantage that any delays on the M25 result in heavy traffic taking the alternative, already quite busy, A25 through part of Godstone.

Very attractive historic buildings in the centre of Godstone surround the green and duck pond. The Tudor and Elizabethan properties are maintained in this conservation area. Intriguing little lanes and alleyways run between them. A pleasant short passage, called Bay Path, runs from the centre and passes through a nature reserve to the church. Here are another collection of old cottages and timber-framed buildings.

Longer walks are via a bridge over the M25 to the steep scarp slope of the North Downs with ancient trackways such as The Pilgrims Way providing access to excellent views. The motorway junction is a distraction but the North Downs Way provides a route away from it into wooded slopes. In the other direction, lanes and footpaths pass through Tilburstowhill Common to the south of Godstone.

South Godstone is, in fact, well to the south and is more recent – another growth around a station (45 minutes to London Victoria).

Blindley Heath

Blindley Heath is further south and is a linear village along the A22, a short distance from South Godstone station.

Much of this area was, in the past, grassland on the clay of this area known as The Weald. Although much of it was ploughed for cultivation of crops, the heath here is a remnant of the old Weald Clay grassland. Good sized individual detached properties are strung out along parts of the straight Roman road, now the A22, that runs from the south to this village and then becomes a quieter lane heading north to Godstone as the A22 branches off to South Godstone.

Bletchingley

Bletchingley (45 minutes to London Victoria) is midway between Godstone and Redhill. This very picturesque village has particularly charming old timber-framed buildings, cottages and tile-hung properties around the old market square, near the partly 11th century church and along the high street. Antique shops and other specialist shops are another attraction of this village. A network of footpaths extend to the north towards the interesting hamlets of Pendell and Brewer Street where substantial properties include some with long histories of association with well known figures such as Ann of Cleeves, one of Henry VIII's wives. Crossing the M25 via a lane provides access to the North Downs and their ancient rights of way.

Nutfield

Nutfield is a village along the A25 from Bletchingley on the way to Redhill station (34 minutes to London Victoria). Fullers Earth was quarried here: a fine clay used in making talcum powder. This has, however, ceased and the environment around the quarries is being improved. One former quarry, now part of Mercer's Park, is used for canoeing and windsurfing. Many houses here are beside the A25, which can get busy and congested at times.

South Nutfield

South Nutfield (40 minutes to London Victoria) is down a lane away from the A25 and has its own station. Part of the village is near to Redhill Aerodrome. Light aircraft and helicopters use it, so it is wise to investigate how much this affects any properties of interest. There are, though, a variety of properties built from the mid 19th century onwards that provide a choice of shapes and sizes, including some large and spacious houses.

Lingfield

49 minutes to London Victoria.

This large, attractive village is south of Oxted and a few miles from East Grinstead, which is just over the boundary into West Sussex.

The conservation area of the village centre has fine old timber-framed buildings. Some of the weatherboarded and tile-hung properties date from the 15th to 18th centuries. A 400-year-old hollow oak tree towers over The Cage, which was used as a 'lock-up' from 1773 to 1882. 'Leafy Lingfield' is a term sometimes used, indicating its position in the middle of wooded countryside.

The town is best known for its Lingfield Park racecourse, which has an all-weather track.

Lingfield has its own station – a short walk from many homes here.

The surrounding countryside is not as hilly as other areas mentioned earlier but still has substantial appeal.

Dormansland

Dormansland (52 minutes to London Victoria) is a close neighbour of Lingfield. This was originally just a few farms and cottages – some unusually small and possibly built originally by squatters on common land several hundred years ago when this was acceptable. The area to the south was chosen for the location of a development, at the end of the 19th century, as 'the new Bungalow Town and Club' now called Dormans Park Estate. This was planned and built with a large plot for each property in a woodland environment. This is an interesting area for seekers of property in or near a rural setting. Dormans station is nearby and the town of East Grinstead is just to the south.

Felbridge

Felbridge is to the southwest of Lingfield and right beside the Sussex border. Plenty of properties backing onto farmland and forest are spread along the A22 and small side roads between Felbridge and Newchapel three miles to the north. These are a short drive from Lingfield station (49 minutes to London Victoria).

A number of mill ponds punctuate the landscape here. The making of iron products, such as cannons and cannon balls, was once a major cottage industry in this area known as the Weald. The ponds would have been used to power watermill hammers. Now they are used for water sports such as sailing and fishing. Hedgecourt Lake is one large example.

Smallfield

Smallfield is in the west of the district and consists mainly of quite recently built property not far from the M23 and the station at Horle. (32 minutes to London Victoria). Nearby Burstow and Horne villages have considerably older properties.

Waverley District including Farnham, Godalming, Haslemere and Cranleigh

This large district, named after Waverley Abbey near Farnham, is an exceptionally attractive area. It is south of the Guildford district and therefore well away from the extensions of Greater London. This district is certainly the place for those who wish to become submerged in wooded and often idyllic hilly countryside. The landscape varies in character from the chalk North Downs near Farnham, through the clay vales formed by rivers and streams, to the sandstone hills – giving plenty of choice.

Farnham, Godalming and Haslemere are substantial towns providing all the usual facilities to the surrounding countryside.

Further south, towards the Sussex border, towns are fewer and the villages smaller and more scattered. This truly rural area may even be a little too remote for some. Obviously it will take longer to reach London from this district – particularly from some villages, which are a substantial drive from a station – but this may be less important for those who are able to spend at least part of their week working at home or who can find employment in Surrey. Railways and main roads do, of course, cross the district but they are not necessarily dual carriageways.

If access to the coast is an attraction, the south of this district is within a fairly short drive – perhaps 40 minutes on a good day – of many beaches and boating facilities on the Sussex coast.

Waverley District Average House Prices

Detached	Semi-detached	Terraced	Flat
497,755	236,713	187,688	185,104

Farnham

56 minutes to London Waterloo.

Farnham has appealing architecture – mainly Edwardian – and is overlooked by a 12th century castle. The town grew where routes converge on a gap in the hills. Not all the roads follow valleys, though. A particularly scenic route runs eastwards from Farnham along the Hog's Back ridge. It is possible to view much of the Waverley district from this ridge and from hills around Farnham.

The roads and the railway provide convenient access to London.

As pleasant as Farnham is, there are many peaceful rural locations around it, particularly to the south, likely to be preferred by seekers of the rural idyll.

Tilford

Tilford village is southeast of Farnham, charmingly situated in the River Wey valley at a medieval bridging point. A huge 900-year-old oak tree is on the village green. Footpaths and lanes through woods lead to Crooksbury Common where the hamlet called The Sands has a number of large properties spread through the trees beside the viewpoint of Crooksbury Hill.

Elstead

Elstead is a few miles further east, again at an arched bridge over the River Wey dating from medieval times. Between the 18th century Elstead watermill and the church are interesting old properties. There is a choice of stations at Farnham, or Godalming and Milford to the east, where the A3 runs northwards.

Godalming

48 minutes to London Waterloo.

This town is south of Guildford and in the River Wey valley. Godalming is an old market town serving a large area of surrounding attractive countryside. The high street has 17th and 18th century buildings including inns and shops. As well as the main Godalming station, Farncombe station (44 minutes to London Waterloo) is to the north and Milford station (54 minutes to London Waterloo) to the south, providing good access to the railway for surrounding areas. The A3 passes to the west and avoids the need to drive through central Guildford on the way to London. The river has locks and weirs, and the associated towpath provides walks out to pleasant farmland. Boating provides alternative access and moorings for boat owners are sometimes available at Farncombe.

Two people responsible for the appearance of some covetable properties and gardens in Surrey and elsewhere lived here: Sir Edward Lutyens, the architect, and Gertrude Jekyll, the gardener.

A good range of properties is to be found here, including terraced cottages and large houses with big gardens. Some of these are in semi-rural settings on the edges of the town – particularly to the south.

Bramley and Wonersh

Bramley and Wonersh are neighbouring settlements to the east of Godalming and beside the former route of the Wey and Arun Canal which is being restored to link the River Thames with the south coast. Plenty of Victorian property – and some older houses of stone, brick, timber and hung tiles – are to be found here. Shalford station (51 minutes to London Waterloo) is to the north, and plenty of hilly countryside is accessible via footpaths. The viewpoint of Chinthurst Hill overlooks the villages and the well-wooded Blackheath is to the east.

Between Godalming and Haslemere are a number of attractive villages and hamlets with plenty of interest to the seeker of a cottage or larger secluded property in idyllic countryside, including Thursley, Wormley, Sandhills, Hambledon and Chiddingfold. These are also within reasonable driving distance of Witley station (57 minutes to London Waterloo) and Haslemere station (57 minutes to London Waterloo).

Haslemere

57 minutes to London Waterloo.

Georgian and Victorian properties are abundant along the roads in the middle of Haslemere, within walking distance of the station. Lines of houses, many of substantial size, stretch out between steep wooded slopes meaning many properties back onto forest or fields. Many houses are in the tile-hung finish typical of this area. Plenty of accessible National Trust forested and hilly countryside extends in all directions from the town.

Hindhead is just to the northwest of Haslemere and also amongst forested hills. Most of Hindhead was built in the late 1890s along the main roads including the A3. The A286 crosses the A3 here and provides a route into Haslemere and its station (57 minutes to London Waterloo).

A good proportion of properties are sizeable and set back in the woods. Well known beauty spots nearby include the Devil's Punchbowl – the very steep-sided end of a valley to the east of Hindhead – and Gibbet Hill where murderers about to be hanged enjoyed good views in several directions. This area is surrounded with footpaths through National Trust landscape of pine woods, heathlands and steep sided valleys.

To the east of Haslemere are some wonderful scattered villages and hamlets such as Chiddingfold and Dunsfold.

Chiddingfold

Chiddingfold has a typical English village green, pond, old church and pub, which is one of several that claim to be the oldest in England. Cottages and other varied property are of interest here, with rolling wooded countryside nearby. The A283, which runs through the village, or alternative country lanes, give access to Witley station (57 minutes to London Waterloo) near Wormley to the north.

Dunsfold

Dunsfold, between Haslemere and Cranleigh, is a linear village with a linear village green along the lane that passes through the village. This results in the many charming properties – some 400 years old – being well spaced out and set beside attractive countryside. This is a quiet and very rural area – idyllic for some; possibly too remote for others. If a substantial drive through country lanes to a station or main road is thought enjoyable at the start and end of journeys, this area will have great appeal.

Alfold

Alfold is a third village to have 'fold' as a name ending. This means 'clearing in a forest' and dates from Saxon times when it was necessary to make a clearing in the dense and continuous forest that covered this area – and most of Britain, for that matter.

Alfold is another particularly attractive village, this time with the A281 nearby – a main road, but a typically winding country road. It is a long drive to a station from here, but once at Guildford the train journey can be comparatively rapid to London.

Cranleigh

Cranleigh is a pleasant town with a variety of comparatively recent property. Some wonderful open and wooded countryside surrounds it, particularly the wooded hills to the north which include Winterfold Wood and Pitch Hill. It does not have its own station and there is a choice of substantial country drives to stations at Ockley (64 minutes to London Victoria) to the east, and Guildford to the north.

Ewhurst

Ewhurst is to the east of Cranleigh and provides a possibly preferable village environment somewhat closer to Ockley station (64 minutes to London Victoria), eastwards along the B2127. 18th and 19th century property is an attraction here. Pitch Hill and Holmbury Hill are accessible via footpaths and lanes to the north. The Greensand Way footpath and others branching from it lead off into picturesque hilly woodland from these hills. To the south and east of Ewhurst are interesting hamlets in linear shapes along country lanes, such as Walliswood, Forest Green and

Pollingford.

SUSSEX

Sussex does not, of course, border Greater London. However, parts of the county have been included as an exception to the rule because they are within a one-hour railway journey of London and have some idyllic rural areas. The most attractive rural areas near those stations are covered in this chapter.

An attraction of the areas of the county covered is their position near to the south coast, with all its traditional attractions of holiday resorts, beaches and watersports as well as being within reach of London. Lovely coastal scenery is also within easy reach.

West Sussex Average House Prices

Detached	Semi-detached	Terraced	Flat
332,328	194,893	163,094	120,879

Extracts from the 2001 OFSTED Report on West Sussex Education Authority:

'West Sussex is the tenth largest education authority nationally. It serves a relatively prosperous and predominantly rural area which also includes several medium sized towns, including seaside resorts and a new town built in the 1950s to house the overspill population from London. A very small number of wards, mostly in the seaside towns, are among the most disadvantaged 15 per cent of wards nationally.

'Standards in schools overall are sound to good. Results are in line with national averages and with similar authorities at Key Stage 1 and 2, and above the national average but in line with similar authorities at Key Stage 3 and 4. Standards are improving in line with the national trend, and with similar authorities at Key Stage 2 and the percentage of pupils attaining five or more passes at grades A*-C at GCSE. In line with the council's priority for excellence in education, very challenging targets have been set which, if met, will bring attainment to the 95th percentile of performance nationally.'

Hospitals

Some of the main hospitals include the following:

(Always check the availability of any particular medical needs carefully when visiting an area.)

Worthing Hospital is a large modern hospital with well-developed facilities.

Princess Royal Hospital in Haywards Heath opened in 1991, serves much of central Susssex along with hospitals in Brighton and includes a special neurosciences unit.

Royal Sussex County Hospital in Brighton will soon include a new children's hospital.

Eastbourne District General Hospital serves the east of Sussex.

East Surrey and Crawley Hospitals overlap Surrey and Sussex in their coverage.

Kent and Sussex Hospital at Tunbridge Wells, Kent serves both counties.

Chichester District

Part of the northern half of this district falls within the one-hour railway journey to London. The valley of the River Rother runs from west to east through this northern section of the district – between the hills of the central part of the Weald and the sharp rise of the scarp slope of the South Downs. The railway line from Petersfield (66 minutes to London Waterloo) to Haslemere (57 minutes to London Waterloo), just over the border into Surrey has stations within reasonable reach of a number of villages in the area, but other parts of the district are rather remote from stations, and journeys towards London – or to rather distant stations along winding roads – could be too time-consuming.

This, though, is an excellent area to become sequestered in extremely rural surroundings, with plenty of forest as well as farmland. The coast is also conveniently accessible for a day out, with all the attractions of resorts, beaches and sheltered boating opportunities.

The A272 runs along the River Rother valley and provides a pleasant east – west country road route from Winchester, eastwards well into East Sussex.

Chichester District Average House Prices

Detached	Semi-detached	Terraced	Flat
398,982	216,494	183,652	139,780

Midhurst

This country market town is where H.G. Wells lived very happily for part of his life and taught at the local school. At Midhurst the River Rother flows past the remains of a castle and the ruins of Cowdray House, famous for the polo matches in its grounds. Quite picturesque timber-framed buildings are to be seen in the pleasant town centre. Properties of various ages are to be found and even the most recent developments are small and close to open countryside, such as Midhurst Common with its network of footpaths. Unfortunately the nearest station involves a substantial drive to reach it. This can, though, be a relaxing journey if not in a hurry, and several stations provide alternatives between Petersfield (66 minutes to London Waterloo) to the west and Haslemere (57 minutes to London Waterloo) to the north.

South of Midhurst, the South Downs Way runs east to west along the high crest of the escarpment, with excellent views.

At the foot of the steep scarp slope is a row of springline villages, so-called because springs providing fresh water rise from the base of the downland chalk. Although rather remote, these may be appealing.

South Harting

This village is west of Midhurst and southwest of Petersfield. Timber-framed houses and thatched cottages line the hill leading to the church with its unusual copper church spire constructed in an octagonal shape.

The South Downs Way and the Sussex Border Path cross up in the nearby downs. These provide routes in all four main compass directions with a choice of steep slopes and extensive views, or more gently sloping ground through woodland and open farmland towards the River Rother.

East Harting

East Harting, not surprisingly, is to the east, below Harting Down which is National Trust land. Here, Beacon Hill provides excellent views and a peaceful wooded haven in the nature reserve. Nearby hamlets and villages of Elstead, Treyford, Didling, Cockling Heyshott and Graffham are spring-line settlements strung out in an attractive position at the base of the Downs.

North of this line of settlements is a scattering of interesting villages in well-wooded countryside, as mentioned below.

Easebourne

Easebourne is just north of Midhurst. Included in its range of properties are very good examples of half-timbered homes.

Lodsworth

Lodsworth, northeast of the town, is a well-established village on the side of the valley of the River Lod. Well-wooded rolling countryside extends in all directions.

Lurgashall

Lurgashall, a few miles further northeast, is a small and covetable group of houses around a green at the junction of several lanes near the excellent viewpoints at Black Down.

Fernhurst

Fernhurst is a larger village on the A286 north of Midhurst. This puts it within easy reach of the station at Haslemere (57 minutes to London Waterloo). The village green has tile-hung cottages overlooking it. Mixed areas of gorse, heather and forest are accessible from the village and the highest point in Sussex at Black Down is in National Trust land to the east.

Trotton and Stedham

Trotton and Stedham are beside the River Rother west of Midhurst and have interesting old bridges over the river. Iping common is to the south of these villages and accessible via several footpaths. Paths and lanes also extend further south to the steep scarp slope of the South Downs.

Horsham District

The district of Horsham is mainly beyond a one-hour train journey to London but the northern end of the district just falls within this category.

This area provides an extension of the lovely rural landscape described in the sections on the neighbouring Surrey districts of Waverley and Mole Valley. To the east, near Gatwick airport, it is important to check the effects of aircraft noise and investigate the current situation concerning possible airport expansion. This seems to change frequently with proposals and counter-proposals announced at frequent intervals. One thing is certain – air traffic is more likely to increase than to decrease over coming years.

Horsham District Average House Prices

Detached	Semi-detached	Terraced	Flat
354,921	200,483	179,864	124,927

Horsham

51 minutes to London Victoria.

This town is at the edge of the one-hour journey to London and exact times depend on which London station is the destination and whether extra is paid to use the Gatwick Express for part of the journey. The A264 dual carriageway links with the M23 towards London, and there is the alternative of the A24 which may look shorter on the map but is likely to be a slower journey northwards.

Plenty of country lanes also provide pleasant parallel routes for those not in a hurry – or to avoid any delays on the main roads.

The town has all the usual facilities to serve the surrounding rural areas, and the central parts show the age of this charming market town. The street known as The Causeway has buildings giving reminders of the town's long history. New housing and council housing has extended the town in some directions. This has led to rather dense built-up areas unlikely to appeal to those seeking a more spacious layout near to countryside. Overall, property here tends to be a little cheaper than in Surrey.

North of Horsham, listen out for noise from Gatwick airport when property-hunting. More recently built aircraft have much quieter engines and can give a misleading impression, so spend some time in the area to hear the true noise level with a variety of aircraft passing over, and decide whether the intrusion would be an irritation.

Lanes to the east of Horsham run into St Leonard's Forest where a hilly and wooded rural environment has scattered properties overlooking the countryside.

Broadbridge Heath

To the west of Horsham, Broadbridge Heath is a village separated from Horsham by the A24, which provides convenient access to rapid road routes to London and to the south coast. The centre has historic old houses, and the extensions of modern housing are on a much smaller scale than in Horsham. This means many properties are within a short walk of open countryside.

Slinfold

A little further west, many interesting secluded properties are strung out along a peaceful lane into the village of Slinfold. Georgian houses are particularly desirable in leafy surroundings here. The tile-hung finish and use of Horsham stone in some properties add to their attraction. The A29 provides a route – partly along a Roman road – to join the A24 on its way to London.

The Downs Link footpath passes Slinfold and follows the route north-westwards of a former old railway track – through rolling countryside and the River Arun valley – to Rudgwick and beyond.

Rudgwick

Plenty of fine old tile-hung houses line the lanes here and southwest to hamlets at Bucks Green and Tisman's Common. A network of lanes and footpaths connect these settlements together, through the River Arun valley.

Warnham

Warnham is close to the northern edge of Horsham. The poet, Shelley was born here in 1792 and lived in the village for the first ten years of his life, attending the local village school. This village provides a rural alternative to the town of Horsham but is within easy reach of its facilities including Horsham stations (51 minutes to London Victoria). Access to A24 and M23 via the A264 is easy from Warnham.

Rusper

Rusper is to the northeast of Horsham with interesting black and white timber-framed properties, a particularly old church and typical centuries old village pubs. The attractiveness of this village and this rural area has to be balanced with some aircraft noise from Gatwick airport to the east of the village.

Crawley

41 minutes to London Victoria.

This New Town is rather more attractive in some parts than the other New Towns built to take overspill population from London in the mid-20th century. More greenery than usual lines some residential streets, and a good variety of housing styles has been used. It has a very large covered shopping centre and a leisure park with plenty of attractions. The station is on the line that has the advantage of a good frequent link to London from Gatwick airport. It is the airport that helps to provide the town's level of full employment. On the other hand, the areas to the north are close to the noise and other pollution of this large and increasingly busy airport.

Again partly because of the airport, there is a rapid road route towards London via the M23. Transport advantages can be enjoyed without actually living in the town and the villages in the surrounding districts of Horsham and Mid Sussex are attractive alternatives for those seeking a rural environment.

Crawley Average House Prices

Detached	Semi-detached	Terraced	Flat
368,826	184,333	147,334	114,776

Mid Sussex

This district includes much beautiful countryside south of Crawley. This takes in plenty of picturesque villages, with village greens, ancient churches and timber-framed properties.

There is a normally quite rapid railway service from Brighton to London Victoria (67 minutes), which helps to extend the area within one hour of London. However, if living in a rural area, it is preferable to be within a few miles of stations in Balcombe (46 minutes to London Victoria), Haywards Heath (46 minutes to London) or Burgess Hill (53 minutes to London Victoria) to keep within an hour's train journey of London. The A23 dual carriageway becomes the M23 and runs parallel with the railway a few miles to the west, also providing a route directly northwards. This road gives the possibility of taking a train from Crawley or a nearby station.

Mid Sussex District Average House Prices

Detached	Semi-detached	Terraced	Flat
371,755	213,849	184,448	133,698

Balcombe

46 minutes to London Victoria.

This picturesque settlement has plenty of listed buildings, Victorian houses and other characterful property within walking distance of the station. Newer housing has been designed in a more spacious and appealing style than most housing estates.

Footpaths and lanes extend into beautiful hilly woodland. To the east is Ardingly Reservoir which is used for sailing and fishing. The village of Ardingley is at the other end of this reservoir.

Ardingly

As well as being a charming village with both old and new property of interest, the village has the showground used for major events such as the South of England agricultural show. The dramatic hilly woodlands include the spectacular grounds of Wakehurst Place, with 500 acres of gardens open to the public. The High Weald Landscape Trail provides a most scenic right of way north and south from Ardingly.

A drive through steeply sloping, winding lanes and over parts of the reservoir leads to the station at Balcombe (46 minutes to London Victoria).

Haywards Heath

46 minutes to London Victoria.

This is a substantial town situated up on heathland. Muster Green is the old centre of the town and good-sized Victorian and Edwardian houses surround an attractive open space here.

More recent property has been built around the station.

The edges of the town have property overlooking pleasant countryside and the headwaters of the River Ouse.

Lindfield is joined to the northeastern side of Haywards Heath. It retains its distinctive character as a typical English village with its wide common, a duck pond and an old church on a hill at the end of the high street. Some very desirable properties ranging from typical tile-hung cottages and houses to more substantial Georgian homes are to be found here.

Scaynes Hill

Scaynes Hill is also on the edge of the town to the southeast – obviously on a hill and with good views from many properties. The Sussex Border path runs through the village providing enjoyable rambles along tracks and through fields. Many substantial detached homes are strung along nearby lanes and along the A272 to overlook North Common at North Chailey with its nature reserve and windmill.

Cuckfield

Cuckfield is west of Haywards Heath and was once on the main route from London to Brighton. This gave it importance as a staging post for horse drawn carriages, which used the numerous old inns. There is a combination of medieval cottages and Victorian property here in amongst a variety of housing types and ages. The fact that the High Weald Landscape Trail runs alongside the village indicates the glorious high-level countryside with plenty of excellent views from many points. In addition to this attraction, there is a choice of driving into Haywards Heath to the station (46 minutes to London Victoria) or along a country road northwards to Balcombe station for access to London (46 minutes London Victoria) or a day out in nearby

Brighton. Alternatively, the A23 is a short drive to the west.

Burgess Hill

This town is about an hour by train to London Victoria and at the limit of coverage of this part of Sussex. It has two stations serving the large area of recent housing estates. It is not as appealing as other settlements mentioned above but it does have good shopping facilities and is within easy reach of gorgeous countryside including the South Downs, which meet the coast as cliffs to the east of Brighton.

East Grinstead

The station at East Grinstead is almost an hour from London Victoria and is, in any case, the end of the line for journeys into this part of Sussex. Originally a country market town, it still serves a large area with its range of shops and services mainly in the attractive old part of the town. More recent growth includes commercial activity and offices. Plenty of very pleasant countryside surrounds the town, and lines of properties are strung out along roads and lanes from East Grinstead, with good access to, and often good views of, the woodland and open countryside. Nearby hunting grounds for more rural homes include the settlements of Ashurst Wood and Forest Row to the southeast.

Beautiful countryside extends to the south into the Ashdown Forest, which includes high heathland as well as forest. Plenty of scattered hamlets and villages surround the forest but they become rather remote for those who need to commute to London.

KENT

A large part of Kent near to London has been developed for housing and industry – particularly near to the tidal River Thames and to the motorways that converge on the Thames crossing. However, beyond this built-up area are some pockets of unspoilt countryside.

The idyllic rural areas are mainly to the south, away from the River Thames. Plenty of wooded and hilly countryside is worth exploring for suitable property, and some of it may be cheaper than in neighbouring Surrey. Unfortunately, much very pleasant countryside lies beyond the one-hour train commuting distance from London. Motorways, including the M2 and M20 and some dual carriageways such as the A21, help to overcome this problem by giving access to a station within reasonable commuting time.

Like Essex, Kent has a long coastline. If this is of particular interest, choosing to live in the rolling countryside between London and the Kent coast could be well worth considering. This makes it easy to reach the sheltered but muddy River Medway estuary for boating activities, the well-known traditional seaside resorts such as Margate and Ramsgate and the cross-channel ferry ports of Dover and Folkestone. The coastal scenery is varied and includes the cliffs of Dover, the extensive shingle and sand beaches to the south and east of the county plus salt marsh wilderness on the less developed parts of the north coast of Kent. Just over the border into Sussex are more attractions such as the charming old town of Rye and the nearby beaches at Camber Sands. Southwest Kent also provides easy access to Hastings, Eastboune and the cliffs at Beachy Head in Sussex.

Kent Average House Prices

Detached	Semi-detached	Terraced	Flat
284,784	169,994	136,074	109,110

Extracts from the 2000 OFSTED Report on Kent Education Authority:

'The provision of education in Kent remains very complex. Kent has 106 secondary schools including three middle schools. There are 33 grammar schools, attended by 32 per cent of secondary pupils. The non-selective schools include wide-ability and high (secondary modern) schools. There is a wide range of secondary school size; 20 per cent of secondary schools have fewer than 600 pupils.

'There has not been much change in the performance of schools since the previous LEA inspection. There remains a very wide variation between the performance of schools across the LEA, including between schools with similar intakes.

'Pupils' attainment at Key Stage 1 in English and mathematics remains close to the national average, but is below the average for statistical neighbours. At Key Stage 2, performance in English and mathematics remains close to the national average and that of statistical neighbours. At Key Stage 3, pupils' attainment in English, mathematics and science is above the national average and similar to that of statistical neighbours.

'At GCSE, the proportion of pupils attaining five or more A*-C grades has improved and is now above the national average, although similar to statistical neighbours. The proportion of pupils attaining five or more A*-G grades and one A*- G grade, and the average points score all remain average.'

Important Note:

As emphasised above, this county has a grammar school and secondary modern school system. It does not have the majority of comprehensive schools to be found in other counties.

Although nearly a third of children are selected for grammar schools, it is important to remember that the rest are not. When visiting schools in areas of interest one should check the current situation carefully. When considering results of schools, remember that the most able pupils go to grammar schools in Kent, in most cases, and this inevitably and unfairly influences comparisons between secondary schools.

Hospitals

Some of the main hospitals include the following:

(Always check the availability of any particular medical needs carefully when visiting an area.)

Darent Valley Hospital in Dartford is a new (year 2000) purpose-built hospital.

Farnborough Hospital at Orpington.

Princess Royal University Hospital is also at Orpington, a new £160 million hospital serving a large area.

Kent and Sussex Hospital at Tunbridge Wells will be replaced by a new hospital in a few years' time.

Maidstone Hospital serves much of west Kent and has particularly well developed cancer treatment facilities.

Medway Maritime Hospital at Gillingham includes well-known baby and child development facilities.

Dartford Borough

45 minutes to London Charing Cross.

Much of the Dartford area is a continuation of the built up area of Greater London and not an obvious area to look for idyllic country locations. Near to the tidal River Thames and the M25 Dartford tunnels and bridge, marsh, industry and housing occupy most of the land. Former chalk quarries have been occupied with developments. To the south of the district, though, the chalk slopes of the North Downs begin to rise and there is some open countryside.

The M25 and the A2 cut through the area but the River Darent valley provides a relatively pleasant environment around the Darenth villages and Horton Kirby. The area is served by two railway lines, and main roads towards London have junctions with the M25.

Dartford Borough Average House Prices

Detached	Semi-detached	Terraced	Flat
321,235	177,561	157,397	128,493

Gravesham Borough

This district includes the large town of Gravesend beside the River Thames. The main rural attraction is the area to the south of the A2 dual carriageway where a substantial section of the North Downs provides some lovely country-side. Housing estates have occupied parts of it along the A227 but there are large hilly and wooded rural areas to the east and west of this road. Two railway lines to London serve the area and the M20 runs past the southern edge of the district. Villages here benefit from easy access to the extensive shopping provision in and between Gravesend and Dartford, including the massive Bluewater Retail Park. Property here may be found somewhat cheaper than other areas around London.

The Channel Tunnel high-speed rail link runs parallel to the A2 and just to the south of it through this district. It passes Gravesend and heads north-westwards between Gravesend and Swanscombe before going under the River Thames. It is important to investigate the effects of this on any property under consideration.

Gravesham Borough Average House Prices

Detached	Semi-detached	Terraced	Flat
270,443	177,039	134,188	97,422

Gravesend

52 minutes to London Charing Cross.

The Thames-side marshes were partly occupied by

industry and Gravesend grew on its location beside this important waterway.

The waterside is interesting with a mixture of old buildings, including pubs and churches as well as defensive and maritime structures in narrow streets.

Victorian and Georgian properties of various sizes are to be found in the town. The most appealing area is likely to be on the southern edges and around the golf course. Unfortunately, the A2 dual carriageway runs close to the southern edge and separates homes from open countryside.

Shorne

This village, to the east of Gravesend, provides welcome relief from the rather bare and built up landscape near the Thames.

Its centuries old timber-framed cottages are of particular interest, among a mixture of other properties of various ages and sizes. Some have panoramic views from hillside locations over the Thames Estuary, with all the shipping going to and from the port at Tilbury. Footpaths and lanes radiate from the village into quite attractive countryside including woodland and open farmland.

The village is separated from the busy A2 by Shorne Wood Country Park, but is only a short drive from this main route to London. A choice exists of taking the train from Gravesend station (52 minutes to London Charing Cross) or the alternative route from Sole Street station (56 minute to London Victoria), an enjoyable few miles away along country lanes.

Cobham

Cobham is a village on the other side of the A2 and again separated from its traffic noise by woodland. The high speed Channel Tunnel railway line runs parallel to the A2 north of Cobham. It is a pretty village on a hill with a variety of properties including some from the 18th century. The old half-timbered pub called the Leather Bottle was used by Charles Dickens as the location for parts of *Pickwick Papers*.

Sole Street station is conveniently near, along a lane, as is the A2 in the other direction.

Tracks, used as rights of way, lead from the village into woodland and over the A2 to Shorne Wood Country Park.

Sole Street

Sole Street (56 minute to London Victoria) is a village south of Gravesend and has its own station within walking distance of the houses here. Its rural location is appealing. Some of the properties on the edge of the village and along the lanes are a good size with ample gardens.

The Wealdway footpath passes through the village and a number of other footpaths connect with it to give plenty of access to the chalk downs rising to the south. Camer Country Park is also in this direction on the other side of the railway.

Meopham

Meopham (53 minutes to London Victoria) also has its own station within walking distance of many properties, although the village is spread for a long distance on the A227. Along this road is a real mixture of centuries old houses and much more recent property. Probably the most attractive spot is beside the green, at the part of the settlement called Meopham Green, near the windmill.

Away from the A227 are a number of attractively located hamlets in amongst the steep hillsides of the North Downs, including Culverstone Green, Priestwood Green, Great

Buckland and Foxendown.

Close to the high crest of the downs is the 20th century development of Vigo Village, with plenty of properties backing onto pleasant woodland beside the North Downs Way, which has excellent views southwards. The M20 cuts through the Downs to the southwest and provides access to London or to stations with short rail journey times to London.

Sevenoaks District including Swanley and Edenbridge

This district borders Greater London but includes plenty of beautiful countryside. It extends far enough from north to south to include parts of the North Downs, the valley to the south of the downs and part of the High Weald of Kent.

A triangle of motorways serve the northern half, including the M26 and M20, which are connected by the M25 as it circles London. This may detract from some rural scenes but the motorways do improve access to many parts of Greater London. Railway journeys are usually rapid from the area.

Sevenoaks District Average House Prices

Detached	Semi-detached	Terraced	Flat
455,364	224,120	173,490	167,739

Swanley

40 minutes to London Charing Cross.

This town is close to Greater London and has grown quickly beside its railway station. It is, though, surrounded by farmland – not the most attractive rural area but reasonably pleasant and with some interesting villages nearby such as Swanley Village, Farningham. Sutton at Hone, Crockenhill, and Eynsford. Swanley and all these villages benefit from being within easy reach of main road routes into London and railway stations at Swanley (40 minutes to London) and Eynsford (45 minutes to London Charing Cross).

Swanley Village

Swanley village is to the north of Swanley town and has a narrow street lined with old and characterful houses. A substantial network of footpaths and lanes give access to some open countryside.

Farningham

Farningham benefits from being bypassed by the A20 and M20 but at the same time being near to a junction between these roads and the M25. Farningham Road station (45 minutes to London Charing Cross) is actually two miles north of Farningham northwards along the A225. Riverside scenes are lovely here beside the 18th century bridge and weather-boarded mill house. Farningham wood has footpaths running through it, and lanes lead southwards to the attractive environment of the River Darent valley as well as the deep valleys and high ridges of the North Downs. The slope of the North Downs rises towards the south with increasingly attractive landscape either side of the valley of the River Darent.

Crockenhill

Crockenhill is separated from Swanley by the A20 and has a number of properties overlooking the surrounding fields. Swanley station (40 minutes to London Charing Cross) is a short distance from here as is the A20 dual carriageway with its M25 and M20 motorway junction.

Eynsford

Eynsford's picturesque narrow stone bridge and ford through the River Darent often feature in pictures on calendars. Timbered houses continue the picturesque theme along the lanes. The charming remains of Eynsford Castle, dating from about 1100, are decorated with an interesting variety of flowering plants. Past the castle and on both sides of the valley, lanes and footpaths extend into Lullingstone park, the magnificent Lullingstone Roman Villa and plenty of excellent rural views from the valley sides. The Romans would have used the rivers Darent and Thames for transport but modern roads and motorways in addition to Eynsford's station now provide easier links with Londinium (45 minutes to Charing Cross).

Sevenoaks

38 minutes to London Charing Cross.

Sevenoaks is surrounded by particularly pretty scenic countryside, especially into the wooded hills to the east and west. The town has a good mixture of old and new. Plenty of interesting specialist shops are there as well as the usual stores and supermarkets.

Rail journeys from the town are usually quite short and rapid into London, and the A21 joins with the motorway system to the west of Sevenoaks.

Plenty of properties on the southern outskirts of the town are likely to interest those who want a view of wooded countryside. The Sevenoaks Common area is charming and is close to viewpoints at Hubbard's Hill. The Greensand Way footpath runs east to west in this area and provides access to much of the best scenery. Knole Park provides plenty of accessible open spaces and gorgeous hilly woodland between Sevenoaks and southeast to the high viewpoint of One Tree Hill. This is a superb area of preserved countryside, with few buildings. This, of course, means there are only a few places to look for property, but when a home can be found for sale, its setting is likely to be most appealing. The hamlets of Stone Street, Godden Green, Lower Bitchet and Bitchet Common may provide opportunities for the lucky house hunter.

Otford

North of Sevenoaks, the River Darent cuts through the North Downs on its way to the Thames estuary. The villages in this, the Darent Gap, are attractive. Otford is at the foot of the steep scarp slope of the downs and at the start of the Gap. The pub and a number of appealing old properties overlook a combination of village pond, 12th century church and large green. Footpaths climb the steep slope north of the village to gain good views of the Kent 'Garden of England' countryside. The North Downs Way and the Pilgrims' Way pass through the village. Otford has a station (49 minutes to London Charing Cross) and is a short distance from M25 motorway junctions.

Shoreham

Shoreham village is also in the Darent valley with a station (46 minutes to London Charing Cross) within walking distance of most properties. The Darent Valley Path provides a way to explore the valley without climbing steep slopes and other footpaths lead to high viewpoints – as rewards for the energetic. The village is a quiet, and even rather remote, riverside haven with a bridge and ford at its centre. No main roads pass through it but Junction 4 of the M25 is only a few miles from the village via the network of narrow country lanes through hills and woodland.

Plenty of very wonderfully located small villages and hamlets are scattered around the Sevenoaks district south of the town, such as Sevenoaks Weald, Penshurst, Goathurst Common and Four Elms. Much scope exists in this area for finding secluded properties in idyllic rural locations. At the same time, the London bound dual carriageway of the A21 and stations at Sevenoaks (38 minutes to London Charing Cross), Hildenborough (44 minutes to London Charing Cross) and Tonbridge are not far away along scenic rural lanes.

Sevenoaks Weald

Sevenoaks Weald is at the foot of the steep greensand scarp slope just south of Sevenoaks. The Greensand Way footpath passes the village and follows the line of the steep slope both to the east and to the west into wonderful countryside with fine views. As the village's name indicates, it is in the Wealden area of Kent where plenty of woodland and rolling, peaceful countryside can sooth away the stress of working in the city. A country lane links with the A21 dual carriageway, which, in turn, links with the motorway system for journeys in all directions. The station at Sevenoaks (38 minutes to London Charing Cross) involves a drive into the town but Hildenborough station (44 minutes to London Charing Cross) is reached via a drive through country lanes to the south.

Penhurst

Penshurst (65 minutes to London Charing Cross) is, perhaps, beyond inclusion within the one hour limit to London (from its own station) but this village has a most attractive setting in the Weald to the south of Sevenoaks. It lies between the River Medway and the River Eden near the grand palace of Penshurst Place. Here, and in other nearby villages and hamlets, are many 16th and 17th century properties, timber-framed or with tile-hung frontages. This area has provided historic settings for film locations.

Chiddingstone

An unusual aspect of the countryside in this area is the occurrence of sandstone rock outcrops such as the Chidding Stone at the tiny village called Chiddingstone, northwest of Penshurst. Chiddingstone has a number of wonderful old buildings including some highly desirable tile-hung and timber-framed cottages.

Goathurst Common, Ide Hill and Toys Hill

Goathurst Common, Ide Hill and Toys Hill to the southwest of Sevenoaks, provide opportunities to look for property set in idyllic forested and hilly countryside, parts of which are owned by the National Trust and are accessible for walks, picnics and excellent views. This area may seem remote and very secluded but country lanes provide an enjoyable drive to the station (38 minutes to London Charing Cross) and motorways around Sevenoaks.

Four Elms

Four Elms is south of Toys Hill and lower down in the Weald. Various types of properties are strung along the roads that cross here and there is scope for finding a home backing on to verdant rolling countryside. Various lanes and footpaths extend into the surrounding area, which includes Bough Beech reservoir. This drowned houses and farmland when it was formed in the 1960s but now adds an attractive feature to the landscape and provides opportunities for fishing and boating – as well as the water everyone needs.

Edenbridge

52 minutes to London Victoria.

This town is midway between London and the south coast and in the centre of the rolling Wealden countryside. The town itself has areas of various qualities. Covetable half-timbered houses are to be seen in the southern part of the town near the River Eden. The straight high street is a Roman road and has some very old coaching inns – possibly over 600 years old. Council estates and some factories occupy the central part of the town. The more interesting properties are on its northern and southern edges, closer to open countryside. North along the B2026 are a string of detached larger properties leading to the attractive village of Crookham Hill. Just north of this village are wooded hills with good viewpoints accessible via several footpaths. Sir Winston Churchill was particularly keen on this area of countryside. Nearby Chartwell was his home.

Edenbridge has two stations and country lanes link with main roads to London.

Westerham

Westerham is to the west of Sevenoaks and north of Edenbridge. This small town has a pleasant atmosphere. Old coaching inns and other old buildings including antique shops and tea rooms surround the small green. Westerham does not have a station so it is necessary to drive to Limpsfield for this facility. The North Downs Way runs east to west nearby and lanes from the A25 into the woods to the southeast are lined with interesting property right up to The Chart, a forested National Trust area high up above the Weald. This area has an interesting mixture of open heath and woodland that extends over the border into Surrey.

The name 'Chart' is the origin of Chartwell – 'the well on the Chart' providing a water supply. Sir Winston Churchill chose this location more for the stunning country views than for the originally rather gloomy Victorian mansion. Such rural views are a major attraction for those escaping from London. The Greensand Way zig-zags through The Chart and other wonderful areas of hilly woodland. Superb views south from the highest points extend across Kent and Sussex.

Tonbridge and Malling District

This district continues the idyllic countryside eastwards from the area to the south of Sevenoaks. Most of the area is between Tonbridge and Chatham. Railways serve the north and south of the district with services to London. Although the central area is some distance from a station, it does have the M20 running through it.

The Channel Tunnel rail link runs across the northern edge of the district, parallel to the M2 just to the southwest of Chatham, and it is important to check how near any interesting properties may be to this new development.

The navigable River Medway is an attraction, although it can be a problem in places if flooding is a threat. This needs to be checked with local authorities and insurance companies.

The steep scarp slope of the North Downs lies across the northern part of the region, providing good views and varied countryside.

Tonbridge and Malling District
Average House Prices

Detached	Semi-detached	Terraced	Flat
330,083	203,752	158,526	128,776

Tonbridge

49 minutes to London Charing Cross.

This attractive old town is at the head of navigation on the River Medway. Notable features include the castle dating from the 12th century and the Victorian cast iron bridge over the river. The castle can be reached via a pleasant and peaceful riverside walk. The old part is centred on the bridging point and the town has grown north and southwards away from here, largely avoiding the flood plain and giving the town an 'hour glass' shape. Until a barrier was built on the river upstream, the high street which crosses the plain was subject to winter flooding. Avoidance of the flood plain means fields from nearby open countryside extend into the centre of Tonbridge, and rural areas are close to much of the town. The footpath known as the Medway Valley Walk runs through the town beside the river, providing easy access to Hayden Country Park and other peaceful areas.

There is also access to peaceful woodland to the south via the High Weald Walk.

The station is centrally placed in Tonbridge, and the A21

dual carriageway is nearby.

Villages are small, quaint and scattered across the scenic area to the north and include Shipbourne, and the interesting scattering of properties around Igtham Common, Borough Green and Trottiscliffe.

Ightham

Ightham is to the north of Tonbridge and is a terrific old village with half-timbered cottages and houses. Oldbury Hill is in National Trust land to the west and has interesting walks in a forested area, which includes an Iron Age fort and Palaeolithic rock shelters. Kemsing station (51 minutes to London Charing Cross) and Borough Green station (55 minutes to London Charing Cross) are nearby and the M26 is accessible via the A25.

Borough Green

Borough Green is to the east of Ightham and provides a more modern range of properties, many of which are within walking distance of the station (55 minutes to London Charing Cross) and yet quite close to some charming rural scenes.

Wrotham

Wrotham (pronounced Rootam) is north of Borough Green with some interesting cottages and newer housing developments close to the North Downs Way and the Pilgrims, Way – providing access to plenty of hilly countryside. Some properties here may be a little too close to the M20 and M26 motorways although, of course, these do help provide routes to London. Borough Green station (55 minutes to London Charing Cross) is just to the south.

Wrotham Heath, Platt and Offham

Wrotham Heath, Platt and Offham are neighbouring villages in splendid countryside with the large Mereworth Woods to the south accessible via the Wealdway and other footpaths and country lanes.

Some larger villages are along the A26 to the northeast of Tonbridge. These are some distance from stations but are nicely situated.

East Peckham and Wateringbury are between Tonbridge and Maidstone, beside the River Medway valley.

East Peckham

East Peckham does not have its own station but Beltring station is nearby (67 minutes to London Charing Cross) and Paddock Wood, three miles south of here, is 53 minutes London Charing Cross. The landscape is comparatively flat here but many lanes lead into more varied countryside and the Medway Valley Walk follows the river through hills to the north.

Wateringbury

Wateringbury has its own station within walking distance of most properties. We are beyond the edge of the one-hour journey range (74 minutes to London Charing Cross) here, though. This may be tolerable for the advantage of living in a rural village with period properties and some good-sized Georgian houses. It could be preferable to drive northwards for a journey of 65 minutes from East Malling station. The Medway Valley Walk follows the river and gives access to miles of glorious countryside.

Wouldham and Halling

In the northwest of the district are substantial housing estates with pockets of hilly countryside between them. Some largely unspoilt villages remain, such as neighbouring Wouldham and Halling. Local stations here are well over one hour to London at 88 minutes, but it may be worth considering the drive to alternative stations further south such as East Malling (65 minutes to London Charing Cross).

Tunbridge Wells

60 minutes to London Charing Cross.

The town of Tunbridge Wells is just within an hour's rail journey of London. The town still has something of an air of quiet gentility despite the office blocks and conversion of some of the large 19th century properties into flats. Plenty of old and characterful property exists here, dating from the development of the town in the 18th century as a spa town, with mineral water people seemed keen to consume despite its taste. The area where the water still trickles out is The Pantiles, with a charming mixture of shops and old buildings dating back as far as the 17th century. Plenty of more modern shops and facilities are northwards, up the hill from The Pantiles. These serve the surrounding area well.

West of The Pantiles is Hungershall Park, and further out is the common with plenty of footpaths and rock outcrops. The largest outcrops are the High Rocks with overhangs, chimneys, crevices and other features enjoyed by rock-climbers who perfect their skills here before tackling more adventurous climbs in mountain areas.

These open areas are within easy walking distance of many properties on the western side of the town and footpaths extend from here into excellent hill and valley landscapes.

Tunbridge Wells Average House Prices

Detached	Semi-detached	Terraced	Flat
389,730	221,001	187,343	157,984

Living in the lovely villages nearby to Tunbridge Wells involves rather more than may be considered a reasonable commuting time to London. Even so, some may be worth considering.

Pembury

Pembury, to the east of Tunbridge Wells and almost joined to it, has plenty of recent housing plus some large Victorian properties near to attractive wooded and hilly countryside.

Matfield

Matfield is further east. Built round a large village green with a well populated duck pond, this village has many nicely preserved Georgian properties overlooking the green. The High Weald Walk runs through the village into sumptuous rural scenery.

Brenchley

Brenchley is almost joined to Matfield and, by contrast, has a *small* village green – a triangular open space – surrounded by weather-boarded houses and pubs. This pretty village and the surrounding hamlets provide a good hunting ground for rural properties in idyllic settings. From Brenchley and Matfield it would be quicker to drive to Paddock Wood station (53 minutes to London Charing

Cross) to the north, rather than to Tunbridge Wells station (60 minutes to London Charing Cross).

Horsmonden

Horsmonden does not have the quaint charm of the villages mentioned above but many of its properties overlook unspoilt countryside, and it has a square green at its centre giving a continental atmosphere. Nearby, the Furnace Pond is in a beautiful location and is formed from old industrial features. The area was, in the past, a centre of iron-working and the artificial areas of water in the Weald of Kent supplied water power for this cottage industry. A footpath runs from Horsmonden to the lake and over the spillway where water cascades down to the basin – the former site of a water-wheel, driving machinery to shape the iron. Commuting time from here is considerable, involving a drive along lanes to Paddock Wood station (53 minutes to London Charing Cross) or Tunbridge Wells (60 minutes to London Charing Cross).

Fordcombe

To the west of Tunbridge Wells, Fordcombe is a village strung out along a narrow country lane with many properties backing onto the valley side of the River Medway offering good views. The Wealdway footpath passes through the village following high ground, while other lanes and paths descend to bridges over the river. Ashurst station (70 minutes to London Victoria) is three miles away down in the valley. Alternatively, Tunbridge Wells station (60 minutes to London Charing Cross) is further to the east.

Ashurst

Ashurst is very small and on a main road (the A264) but is pleasantly located in a valley near a weir pool on the

Sussex border. It has a station (70 minutes to London Victoria) within walking distance of most homes here.

Speldhurst

Northwest of Tunbridge Wells, Speldhurst is a neatly arranged village up on a hill. A mixture of properties are of interest here and the pub – the George and Dragon – claims to date from 1212. The High Weald Way meets other footpaths here to give access to attractive and varied countryside. The High Brooms Station (56 minutes to London Charing Cross) north of Tunbridge Wells, is to the east along country lanes.

Bidborough

Bidborough is north of Tunbridge Wells and has large houses with excellent views, from a ridge, over the nearby valleys. The old part of the village is down a slope from the ridge with cottages arranged around the attractive old church. The Wealdway passes the church and goes on into wooded valleys. High Brooms station (56 minutes to London Charing Cross) is a short drive towards Tunbridge Wells.

Medway Towns

As the name of this district suggests, this is an area of towns rather than idyllic rural locations. As interesting as many parts of the district are, such as the old area of Rochester (58 minutes to London Charing Cross) and locations overlooking the River Medway valley and the coast, those seeking the most attractive rural environments may prefer to look beyond the edges of these towns. This, though, leads mainly to places beyond what might be considered as reasonable commuting time to London.

Medway Towns Average House Prices

Detached	Semi-detached	Terraced	Flat
232,451	151,514	114,865	97,312

The area around Rochester and Chatham is Dickens country. Charles Dickens spent much of his life here and it provided settings for some of his novels. He enjoyed walks up to Gads Hill, where he lived for the last fourteen years of his life, to the northwest of Rochester. Much of the area has been built up since then but quite pleasant countryside still extends as a peninsula between the River Medway and the River Thames estuary.

Rochester

Rochester (58 minutes to London Charing Cross) has charming old streets full of specialist shops, a quite small but splendid cathedral and a castle overlooking the river. Appealing Elizabethan and Georgian properties are to be found here as well as plenty of Victorian terraced houses. The surroundings include rather drab industrial areas and housing estates before one reaches open countryside. However, there are some villages to explore not too far away.

Higham

Higham station (65 minutes to London Charing Cross), northwest of Rochester, serves the old part of Higham village near the Thames marshes. Higher up, the more recent Higham housing expands southwards towards Rochester.

Upnor Villages

On the banks of the tidal River Medway, the attractive Upnor villages have weatherboarded houses, an Elizabethan castle and a slipway into the river. The estuary here was, for many centuries, used for sheltering, supplying, building and repairing naval warships. The former naval dockyards on the other side of the river have been renovated and are now a large museum area, which provides an interesting view over the water from the villages and footpaths on nearby Tower Hill. The sheltered estuary is accessible for boating activities, and facilities for mooring and maintaining boats are available.

Hoo

Hoo is further northeast and is mainly an area of modern housing estates, although there are some Georgian buildings near the original centre.

Cliffe and High Halstow

The villages of Cliffe and High Halstow are rather remote – out on the peninsula jutting into the Thames Estuary. As it has a sparse population and flat land, the area has been considered as a location for a new 'London' airport on several occasions but currently the emphasis seems to be on the expansion of Stansted Airport in Essex. This part of Kent has a mixture of marshes, flat open spaces, glorious skyscapes and views out to sea.

Appendix 1

This is a very subjective indication of what might be considered 'the best' rural locations in each category. Many may feel other locations should be included but the intention is to give a starting point for those in search of a particular aspect of country life.

15 Best Locations for Rural Seclusion

The River Stour valley in north Essex near to the Suffolk border.
The Dengie peninsula on the Essex coast west of Maldon.
Little Baddow, Essex.
Hertfordshire's northeast rural corner.
Villages to the northeast of Great Missenden and west of High Wycombe, Buckinghamshire.
Mattingley to the west of Hartley Wintney, Hampshire.
Worldham villages east of Alton, Hampshire.
Villages west of Petersfield, Hampshire.
Southwest of Shere, Surrey.
West of the railway between Horley and Redhill, Surrey.
Southwest of Oxted hamlets near Tandridge village, Surrey.
Area surrounding Godalming, Surrey.
Villages near Haslemere, Surrey.
Slinfold area west of Horsham, Sussex.
South of Sevenoaks, Kent.

25 Best Locations for Character Property

Thaxted and Saffron Walden area (Uttlesford District in Essex).

Finchingfield, Essex.

Coggeshall, Essex.

Therfield, Hertfordshire.

Graveley, Hertfordshire.

Willian, Hertfordshire.

Aldbury, Hertfordshire.

Beaconsfield area of Buckinghamshire.

Marlow, Buckinghamshire.

Whitchurch, Buckinghamshire.

Crondall, Odiham and Hartley Wintney area of Hampshire.

South Warnborough, Hampshire.

Overton, Hampshire.

Old Basing, Hampshire.

Selbourne, Hampshire.

Buriton, Hampshire.

Cobham, Surrey.

Chobham, Surrey.

Shere, Surrey.

Godstone, Surrey.

Bletchingley, Surrey.

Lingfield, Surrey.

Shorne, Kent.

Otford, Kent.

Ightham, Kent.

15 Best Semi-Rural Locations for Waterside Property

On the coast:
Mersea Island, Essex.
Maldon, Essex.
Heybridge, Essex.
Maylandsea, Essex.
Bradwell-on-Sea, Essex.
Burnham-on-Crouch, Essex.

Beside waterways:
Chelmsford, Essex – to the east, beside the River Chelmer Canal.
Sawbridgeworth, Hertfordshire – River Stort Canal.
Marlow, Buckinghamshire – River Thames.
Windsor, Berkshire and other nearby locations on the River Thames.
Aldermaston, Berkshire – and other nearby locations on the Kennet and Avon canal.
Weybridge, Surrey – River Thames and River Wey.
Godalming, Surrey – River Wey.
Guildford, Surrey – River Wey.
Upnor, Kent and other locations upstream on the River Medway.

5 Best Areas for Hilly Countryside and Good Views

Most good atlases will show the precise areas of the following in relation to rural towns and villages.

Chiltern Hills mainly northwest of Greater London.
North Downs chalk escarpment in Kent and Surrey.

The greensand ridges south of the chalk North Downs in Hampshire, Surrey and Kent.
The central Weald's higher parts in southern Surrey and Kent and on the Sussex border.
South Downs chalk escarpment in Hampshire and Sussex.

Appendix 2

London main line terminuses and travel times

The list of stations and journey durations from attractive rural locations to London mainline terminuses may be helpful, bearing in mind the notes below.

Journey durations shown in minutes next to many towns and villages give an approximate indication for a typical train journey to a mainline London terminus. This is based on the online timetable for a journey departing between 8 and 8.30 a.m. on a weekday and provides a rough guide only. Timetables are often changed so the current situation should be checked when considering the area as a place to live. The website **http://www.nationalrail.co.uk** can be used to find up-to-date details of times and routes.

The terminus indicated is often *one of several alternatives* so it is important to investigate the best route to take. For example, London Bridge may be an alternative to Victoria station and Cannon Street an alternative to Charing Cross. Obviously, do not base a final decision on where to live solely on the approximate journey details provided below.

It is advisable to try the journey one weekday morning and ask some regular passengers about the current situation concerning the quality of the service.

Approximate minutes for journey duration from locations with mainline stations covered in Part Two – near to attractive rural towns and villages

Charing Cross

Beltring	67
Borough Green	55
Dartford	45
East Malling	65
Eynsford	45
Gravesend	52
High Brooms	56
Higham	65
Hildenborough	44
Kemsing	51
Otford	49
Paddock Wood	67
Penshurst	65
Rochester	58
Sevenoaks	38
Shoreham	46
Swanley	40
Tonbridge	49
Tunbridge Wells	60
Wateringbury	74

Euston

Berkhamsted	35
Hemel Hempstead	30
Rickmansworth	26
Tring	40
Watford	24

Kings Cross

Baldock	46
Borehamwood	21
Brookmans Path	37
Harpenden	32
Hatfield	40
Hitchin	35
Knebworth	34
Letchworth	36
Potters Bar	32
Radlett	23
Royston	46
St. Albans	24
Stevenage	29
Welwyn Garden City	30

Liverpool Street

Audley End	62
Battlesbridge	47
Billericay	38
Bishop's Stortford	47
Braintree	63
Brentwood	38
Burnham-on-Crouch	68
Chelmsford	39
Colchester	60
Epping	38
Harlow	38
Hatfield Peverel	42
Hertford East	44
Hockley	48
Ingatestone	36
Kelvedon	51
Newport	59
Romford	27
Roydon	40
Sawbridgeworth	55

Shenfield	30
Southend-on-Sea	60
South Fambridge	47
Stansted Mountfitchet	58
Ware	40
Witham	50
Wivenhoe	65
Woodham Ferrers	54

Marylebone

Amersham	37
Aylesbury	59
Beaconsfield	38
Chalfont and Latimer	33
Gerrards Cross	33
Great Missenden	44
Haddenham	53
High Wycombe	38
Little Kimble	61
Monks Risborough	57
Princes Risborough	50
Saunderton	45

Paddington

Aldermaston	54
Bourne End	53
Burnham	31
Cookham	50
Eton	49
Iver	30
Maidenhead	28
Marlow	64
Midgham	58
Pangbourne	55
Reading	30
Slough	33
Theale	49

Twyford	43
Wargrave	45
Windsor	30

Victoria

Ashurst	70
Balcombe	46
Banstead	38
Betchworth	56
Bletchingley	45
Brighton	67
Burgess Hill	53
Caterham	43
Crawley	41
Dorking	53
Dormansland	52
Earlswood	44
East Grinstead	56
Edenbridge	52
Gomshall	63
Haywards Heath	46
Holmwood	60
Horley	32
Horsham	51
Hurst Green	37
Leatherhead	45
Lingfield	49
Meopham	53
Ockley	64
Oxted	38
Redhill	34
Reigate	50
Salfords	47
Sole Street	56
South Nutfield	40
Warlingham	35
West Humble	51

Waterloo

Addlestone	51
Aldershot	49
Alton	71
Ascot	46
Bagshot	65
Basingstoke	45
Bentley	62
Bracknell	64
Bramley	59
Brookwood	37
Byfleet	33
Camberley	71
Chertsey	54
Chilworth	55
Cobham	35
Effingham	38
Egham	43
Farnborough	43
Farncombe	44
Farnham	56
Fleet	49
Frimley	75
Godalming	48
Guildford	41
Haslemere	57
Hook	55
Horsley	42
Liphook	67
Liss	73
Micheldever	56
Milford	54
Oxshott	31
Petersfield	66
Shalford	51
Shepperton	51

Index 1

Alphabetical index of place names

Kimpton: 120

Kings Langley: 136

Kings Walden: 119

Kingsclere: 204

Kingsley: 208

Kingswood: 253

Knebworth: 121

Knowl Hill: 169

Laleham: 220

Lane End: 154

Latimer: 149

Leatherhead: 246

Lee Common: 151

Leigh: 255

Lemsford: 124

Letchworth: 116

Lightwater: 233, 235

Lilley: 119

Limpsfield: 257

Limpsfield Chart: 257

Lindfield: 282

Lingfield: 255, 261

Liphook: 213

Liss: 212

Little Baddow: 71

Little Chalfont: 148

Little Gaddesdon: 137

Little Kimble: 157

Little Leighs: 80

Little Marlow: 155

Little Offley: 118

Little Totham: 72

Little Waltham: 71

Little Warley: 93

Little Wymondley: 120

Littleton: 221

Littlewick Green: 169

Lodsworth: 275

London Colney: 128

Long Crendon: 162

Long Sutton: 192

Loudwater: 133

Loughton: 89

Lower Bitchet: 295

Lower Froyle: 209

Lurgashall: 275

Lyne: 225

Maidenhead: 166

Maldon: 72

Malling District: 299

Manuden: 88

Mapledurwell: 201

Margaretting: 94

Marlow: 154

Marlow Bottom: 155

Matfield: 304

Mattingley: 195

Mayford: 232

Maylandsea: 74

Medstead: 207

Medway Towns: 306

Meopham: 291

Micheldever: 199

Mickleham: 248

Mid Holmwood: 249

Mid Sussex: 280

Midgham: 184

Midhurst: 274

Mole Valley District: 246

Molesley: 229

Monk Sherborne: 202

Monks Risborough: 157

Wallington: 115

Walliswood: 250

Walters Ash: 153

Waltham Abbey: 89

Waltham St Lawrence: 169

Walton on the Hill: 253

Walton-on-Thames: 226

Wanborough: 244

Ware: 109

Wargrave: 180

Warlingham: 256

Warnham: 278

Warren Corner: 193

Wateringbury: 302

Watership Down: 198, 204

Watford: 132

Watling Chase: 101, 131

Waverley District: 263 4

Welham Green: 125

Welwyn: 122

Welwyn Garden City: 122

West Clandon: 239

West End: 236

West Green: 195

West Horsley: 239

West Meon: 214

West Mersea: 78

West Worldham: 208

Westcott: 250

Westerham: 298

Westhumble: 248

Westmill: 107

Weston: 115

Wexham: 144

Weybridge: 226

Wheathampsted: 129

Wheatley: 209

Whitchurch: 160

White Waltham: 169

Whitwell: 120

Wickham Bishops: 81

Widdington: 88

Wildhill: 126

Willian: 117

Winchendon: 162

Winchester: 188, 197, 199, 206, 240, 248, 273, 333

Winchfield: 235

Windlesham: 235

Windsor: 167-70

Windsor and Maidenhead District: 166

Winnersh: 179

Witham: 81

Wivenhoe: 78

Woking: 231

Woking Borough: 231

Wokingham: 177-8

Woldingham: 256

Woldingham Garden Village: 256

Wonersh: 266

Wood Street: 244

Woodside: 126

Woolhampton: 184

Wormley: 266, 267

Worplesden: 232

Wouldham: 303

Wrays: 255

Wraysbury: 173

Writtle: 70

Wrotham Heath: 302

Wyck: 209

Wycombe District: 152

Yateley: 194

Index to Illustrations

Section 1

11b) Terling village green in Essex.

12a) Timber-framed houses near open countryside at Saffron Walden, Essex.

12b) Saffron Walden market in Essex.

13a) Timber-framed and brick built cottages in Saffron Walden, Essex, close to open countryside.

13b) Much Hadham, Hertfordshire, cottages backing onto open countryside.

14a) Much Hadham, Hertfordshire, variety of cottages.

14b) Timber-framed house backing onto open countryside, Much Hadham, Hertfordshire.

15a) Little Hadham village green overlooked by cottages close to Hertfordshire countryside.

15b) Country home at Little Hadham, Hertfordshire, backing onto Chiltern hillside.

16a) Substantial property backing onto open countryside at Little Hadham, Hertfordshire.

16b) Brent Pelham village, Hertfordshire, church and thatched cottages overlooking rolling countryside.

Section 2

17a) A classic thatched cottage at Sawbridgeworth, Hertfordshire.

17b) Village houses at Sawbridgeworth, Hertfordshire.

18a) Canal and countryside overlooked by waterside properties at Sawbridgeworth, Hertfordshire.

18b) New flats overlooking the canal and countryside at Sawbridgeworth, Hertfordshire.

19a) New flats overlooking the canal at Sawbridgeworth, Hertfordshire.

19b) Riverside walk near Sawbridgeworth, Hertfordshire.

20a) Pub and cottages overlooking the village green at Therfield, Hertfordshire.

20b) Country house and The Chiltern Way footpath at Kelshall, Hertfordshire.

21a) Village well structure and community noticeboard at Anstey, Hertfordshire.

21b) Idyllic scene in Buckland village, Surrey.

22a) Village property backing onto open views of countryside at Buckland, Surrey.

22b) Buckland village properties overlooking pond and green with Surrey countryside at rear.

23a) The River Thames at Weybridge, Surrey.

23b) View of Kent and Sussex from a home on a hill.

24a) Tile hung properties in Bletchingley, Surrey.

24b) Bletchingley in Surrey.

25a) Village post office and cottages at Bletchingley, Surrey.

25b) Cottages and country lanes at the village of Shere, Surrey.

26a) Cottages and riverside path at Shere in Surrey.

26b) Village church and cottages at Shere in Surrey.

27a) Pub at night beside Pyrford Lock on the River Wey Canal, Surrey.

27b) Stone built home at Toys Hill overlooking the Weald of Kent and Surrey.

28a) The village of Abinger Hammer in Surrey.

28b) Cottages and country lane at the village of Abinger Hammer, Surrey.

29a) Home on a hill with a view over Kent and Sussex.

29b) Secluded bungalow – a renovation project near Sevenoaks, Kent.

30a) Converted oast house, Westerham, Kent.

30b) Hill top footpath and bridleway for horses and cyclists near Goathurst Common, Kent.

31a) View enjoyed by properties near One Tree Hill, Kent.

31b) The village of Shorne, Kent.

32a) Horse riders pass a converted oast house at Ightham, Kent, riding into open countryside beyond.

32b) Houses on Ide Hill with country views in Kent.